THE HEARTBEAT OF GOD BOOK 3

"The Fiery Flame Of Love"

By Charles W. Warner

First printing:
Charles W. Warner Books

Charles W. Warner Books

Foreword

When Charles asked me to help on this book I was excited and a little scared. It is a big responsibility and I want to make sure it is done right. Both for Charlie and for God. It has been quite the learning experience and working with my husband has been a great part of it. We haven't been married that long but have known each other since 1980. I really stand behind my husband and all that he does. He is the real thing and I believe in him. I felt this way even before we dated. I have never done anything quite like this before, yet it is a challenge and something that I really want to be a part of. Charles has already written three books. The two "Heartbeat Of God" books and an earlier one years before. I am so blessed to have been a part of helping put together and to be a part of this book. This latest installment in the "Heartbeat Of God" collection is by far as inspirational and heartfelt as you have come to expect from Charles. Book Three is a wonderful collection of heartwarming stories, thoughts and poetry poured out from God's heart and put to pen and paper for you. A gift to treasure and to share with those you love. As you read and open your heart to what God has given us through Charles, I pray that you will feel His presence and love as we have in working on this series. It has taken us a little bit longer than we had planned to complete. The holidays, family and vacation as well as our own wedding this past December have kept us busy. This has been a beautiful journey and now we present you with *The Heartbeat Of God- Book 3,"The Fiery Flame Of Love"*. _Connie Warner

Isaiah 55:11 KJV

So shall my word be that goeth forth out of my mouth: it shall not return unto me void, but it shall accomplish that which I please, and it shall prosper in the thing whereto I sent it. "I speak the Word of God, God's personal promise to me, (not my opinion not your theology), and it always produces good fruit running over."

Introduction by Charles W. Warner

Why did I write this book? First of all I did not write this book. No I am not a thief, I did not steal this. God wrote this book via my hands, my heart and my mind. For God is truly the author and I am the co-author.

Why did I write this book? Beyond having more hope, love, dreams, prayers and poetry to share. I pray, I proclaim, I prophesy that I wrote this so that God would consume my enemies, our enemies and their families and friends with an all-consuming fire.

I call forth an army, a legion, of angels to come forth for this assignment. I call forth the King of Kings, the King of Glory, The Lord of Hosts to come forth and lead this army. This war, this righteous war, to save souls, to awaken the sleeping giants. To call the foolish to have eyes to see and ears to hear, a mouth to talk and feet to walk.

Holy Ghost set the roots of wickedness on fire. Shine the light of our Lord Jesus in the enemy's camp. Scatter the darkness, shine Jesus shine. Set souls ablaze with the love of their lives, the love of their hearts. Turn up the heat on the worst, the darkest, the most wicked of the wicked, the leaders of the lost, turn up the heat with no limits until they drop on their knees in tears with raised hands and humbled hearts. Crying out to Jesus, "Save my poor soul. Save me from me. Save my family and my friends from me. Shine your pure light in this darkness. Shine your pure light in our hearts. Shine your pure love, your grace, your glory. Redemption story, lives here."

Holy Ghost draw hungry hearts to Jesus, like a moth to a flame. Hearts are hungry and only Jesus can satisfy a hungry heart, hearts as dry straw. Holy Ghost, you are a fire. I am a live wire. God live, work and love through me. This world is shifting, sinking sand. Jesus

and only Jesus is the solid Rock of Ages. This world is the Titanic and Jesus is The Ark.

I dedicate this book and all books I write to God the author and finisher of this book. The Heartbeat of God~ What I love about writing for God is ~ What I write is sealed with His heart to last beyond time into eternity~ To celebrate Jesus now and in that great forever more. God is the Author I am the co-author.

I lay my life down, I lay my books down that God may pick them up to His glory for God's Glory is my heart's delight. I write as God's Heart Scribe meaning I write the cry, the passion, the desire, and the fire of God's heart to celebrate Jesus and love one another. "Speak truth live love".

This book is the Revelation the heartbeat of God that God gave to me that I now share with you.

Charles W. Warner

Table Of Contents

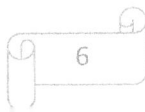

(Redemption Story)

Resting in the arms of my beloved.
I do not want the crown without the King of glory.
I do not want to write my own life's story.
I do not want a robe of my own righteousness.

Jesus is my joy, my bliss, my righteousness.

Take the whole world, but give me my Jesus.
In the arms of Jesus I am loved.
In the arms of Jesus I am found.
In knowing Jesus I know who I am

"I am my Beloved and he is mine"

Charles W. Warner

(Good News)

Love those who hurt you, give Living Water to your enemies and watch the ravenous wolves drink deep of this Living Water. I drink deep of this Living Water. I bow before my King Jesus letting His love His Blood wash over me. I once was lost but now I am found. I once was blind, but now I see. It's Jesus blood that cover me. It's Jesus love that carries me. I love my Lord Jesus. I feed His sheep, of whom I am now one. Blessed be God forever and ever more.

Job 22:28

Thou shalt also decree a thing, and it shall be established unto thee: and the light shall shine upon thy ways.

Charles W. Warner

(Crown of Glory)

A story about God placing a golden crown with rubies and emeralds on my head-

God thank you for this crown but why did you place this on my head? Because you are a king in my courts in My Kingdom. King Charles you have been writing for me for years now, you are my Heart Scribe.

Charles you wear a crown with a kingly anointing for you have been praying, crying out, proclaiming, prophesying my heart for some time so for all time and forever in eternity. Charlie my dear Son, I call you a King.

I wear my crown proudly because I am most proud of my God and King of Kings.

I wear my crown as a servant king for Jesus, you are the servant King.

I wear my crown humbly and meekly as a gentle lamb.
I wear my crown boldly and strong as a mighty lion.

"I am my Beloved and he is forever mine."

I wear my crown, I wear my signet ring, to signify who I am and of whom I am. I belong to the Great I AM, the King of glory!

I wear my robe of righteousness presented to me by the Prince of Peace. My Jesus wore a crown of thorns that I may wear a robe of righteousness.

Charles W. Warner

"Jesus wore a crown of thorns that we may wear a robe of righteousness. He became sin who knew no sin that we may become his righteousness. Love so amazing." 2 Corinthians 5:21

(Dear Jesus)

Dear Jesus I want you to know your scars are most beautiful.

"Jesus is the Word made flesh. Jesus is love manifest"

Charles W. Warner

(Jesus My Hearts' Delight)

Jesus you are my freedom.
My passion.
My prize.
Jesus just to gaze in your eyes.
Jesus you are my Lord.
My life.
My love.

Jesus you are my one desire.
Jesus you are the fire
that burns in my bones
that burns in my heart.
Jesus just to fall at your feet means everything to me.

Dear Jesus you call nature your home and you call me your Beloved One. Jesus I call you my Hearts' Delight because you are, you know. Jesus you dance with me, you sing with me, you laugh with me you hear my silent cry. Jesus you are my lullaby. Jesus you are my life. You are my world. Jesus I am forever thankful that you have your fingerprints all over my heart. .
J E S U S ~ What a beautiful name.

(Life Questions)

Can you answer these questions?

Who am I?
Where do I come from?
Why am I here?
Where am I going?

There is more to this life then living and dying trying to make it on my own. Seize the day seize whatever you can for life slips away like hour glass sand...

"I am here to know God and make him known"

Worship God

Celebrate Jesus
Love one another
Led and fed by Fire by Holy Ghost.
Charles W. Warner

(Banqueting Table)

Welcome to my Father's banqueting table. I am the Bread and the Wine. This Wine over flows and this Bread has already been broken. Beloved you are most welcomed here. I am for you, this covenant blood is for you. I Am the Living Water. I Am the Bread of life. Come eat, drink, Over flow, take what you will and give freely for I am yours and you are mine.

Charles W. Warner

(The Good, The Bad and The Best)

Bad- Gossip, backbiting, lying.
Repeating bitter, hateful, demonic rumors.
Loving to spread discord and division.
Talking, preaching at, not to, not wanting to listen or learn.

A motor mouth. A beady eyed, long nosed talkaholic. Needing the accolades of others. Not able to see past their nose.

Good- Talking with someone not at someone.
Loving to listen and learn.
Giving Godly wise advice.
Giving, sharing. Give and take. Love & laughter.

Best- Praying with others. Interceding for others, prevailing in prayer.
Praying in silence, not needing the applause of man.
God so loves me so that I may truly love you.
Oh how I love Jesus, because He first loved me.

Charles W. Warner

I delight greatly in the Lord; my soul rejoices in my God. For he has clothed me with garments of salvation

Isaiah 61:10

(Garments Of Salvation)

I delight greatly in the Lord; my soul rejoices in my God. For he has clothed me with garments of salvation.

My Lord loves me. He is love and He has anointed me with praise.

Behold he has placed a new song in my heart. He is my heart's song.

He is my dance, my sweet romance, He is my passion, my desire, the fire that burns in my bones.

Adonai has saved me from me and he has redeemed me from all that would keep me from Him.

My Jesus wore a crown of thorns that I may wear a robe of righteousness.

The Lord liveth and blessed be the Rock of my salvation.

Behold my Redeemer lives and he delights in me!

Charles W. Warner

(Covered by Love)

What do I want to do?
I want to listen to silence and be happy to hear it.
I want to do nothing because I can.
I want to not have a cell phone in my pocket or my hand, a
computer staring at me, a TV in front of my face or a phone ready
to ring.

I want to lay in the green grass
I want to feel sunlight shining on my shoulders
I want to see a lonely white cloud floating high in the blue sky.

I want to hear nature, a bull frog, a cricket, the call of an owl. I want
to hear a gentle breeze blowing though the leaves of the mighty
oak trees.

I want to rest on a hill side smelling beautiful wild flowers, eating
wild berries. I want to hear nature call my name.

I want and will walk in the cool of the day with my Creator, my
Beloved. I will sing and dance in the noon hour. I will sing and dance
in the heat of the day with my Daystar for Jesus is my joy all day
long.

I will sleep sweet sleep in the still of the night. I sleep in the arms of
Holy Ghost. Yes I am covered by the wings of a snow white dove,
covered by love.

God is my ever present help the one I love, the one who loves me.
And so I rest in nature with the
Creator thereof. Amen

Charles W. Warner

(God's Home Sweet Home)

What we allow in our home will determine the atmosphere we abide in.

This home is God's home sweet home.

This home is a dwelling place for Jesus.

This home is the habitation of the Holy Ghost.

The Word of God is the truth, the standard of my home.

I plead the Blood of Jesus over my home.

My home is a house of prayer.

This home is a place of rest, peace, joy and love.

This home is where we feed on the fruit of the Holy Spirit.

Joy, love & laughter live here because God calls my house home.

Prophesy, proclaim~

Jesus in my house

Jesus in your house

Jesus in the work house

Jesus in the school house

Jesus in the White House

Jesus in the church house

Charles W. Warner

As for me and my house, we will serve the Lord. Josh 24:15

This is what I seek: That I may dwell in the house of the Lord all the days of my life. Ps. 27:4

The Lord blesses the home of the righteous. Prov. 33:3

God's intimate friendship blessed my house. Job 29:4

*Surely your goodness and love will follow me
all the days of my life, and I will dwell in the house of the Lord forever.
Ps. 23:6*

*(This is the house that God built.) Psalm 127:1
Except the Lord build the house, they labour in vain that build it: except the Lord keep the city, the watchman waketh but in vain.*

(Nancy has the big hair, Amy is the little girl.)

(Amy's Song)

~A story of a visit to Heaven & a talk with Jesus~

When my Sister's daughter, Amy, was 5 years old she was in the bathroom. Her Mom, Nancy, heard a loud sound and my sister knew her daughter fell and hit her head!!! Nancy knew from the Holy Spirit that Amy had died so she prayed something like... this- Jesus please bring Amy back to me, she's just a baby and I need her I love her. Then a while after that Amy walked out of the bathroom with a story to tell.

Amy told it like this... I was in a bright place with people all around. They were nice people, smiling at me. Then there came a man who looked at me, he was so nice and so sweet that I told him I wanted to stay with him but he said- Amy My dear child your Mother is praying for you. It's not your time yet to be here. You have work to do and love to give. Bye for now my precious, adorable princess I will see you soon.

Written by Charles W Warner as told by Nancy Vikouski and Amy (Vikouski) Ebersole

Are You Hooked On Jesus?

(I'm hooked on Jesus)

I'm addicted to Jesus because ~Jesus is most contagious & Holy Spirit is the career~

You are a Son of God building the Kingdom, a child of light or else you are a spawn of darkness, a child of darkness. Are you ushering in the return of King Jesus or the Anti-Christ?

I want to be beautiful! I want my life to be beautiful! If there is anything beautiful about me it's all about you Lord Jesus for you are The Beautiful One!!!..

Charles W. Warner

(The Lion and the Lamb)

J.E.S.U.S.

He Came, He Died, He Arose, He Ascended, He's Coming Back...

(This Is My Daddy)

When we all get to heaven,
what a day of rejoicing that will be!
When we all see Jesus,
we'll sing and shout the victory!

Dad will have a good old time home in Heaven~
In that land that is fairer then day.
In that land where the Lamb is the Light.
In that great forever more.

My Dad has the hands of a Master Carpenter.
My Dad has the hands of a Master Gardener.
My Dad has a cute smile and a sweet, kind heart.
My Dad has cool, holy, blue jeans.

God is a Gardener.
Jesus is a Carpenter.
Holy Ghost is a Wind of Fire.

Someday Mom will say to Dad~ What took you so long, you old
goat?! lol... words of endearment.

Dear Father God, please bless my dear Daddy. Jesus abide here in
our hearts and home until we see you face to face, heart to heart,
until I dance with my Mommy on streets of pure gold.

Amazing Grace

When we've been there ten thousand years,
bright shining as the sun,

we've no less days to sing God's praise,
than when we'd first begun.

Charles W. Warner

(Breath of Life)

Come away my love, my dove, cast all your cares on me for I care for you. I love you my Beloved Bride, my one and only. My Dear

Beloved Bride we are one, your heart is mine and my heart is yours. Lord Jesus I need you more than yesterday, I need you more than words can say. Take the whole world but give me my Jesus.

Healing Rain, Living Water, wash over me. You are my Light, my Love, and my Lord. When the devil reminds me of my past, he is reminding me that you are my Savior of all, My Redeemer of all, My All in All. My Adonai when I cry. You turn my tears of sorrow into tears of joy. Shiloh I know you will never let me go for "I am my Beloved and He is mine". Immanuel it is well with my soul, because you are the Love of my life.

Charles W. Warner

(Bottled and Sealed with Love)

I am at Jesus' feet at the cross crying.
I look up at Jesus as He looks at me with deep beautiful eyes. He takes my breath away and yet at the same time He is the air I breathe~ with endless perfect love He says~ My dear Beloved Bride this blood, my blood is for you. Even as Jesus says this His precious blood is flowing down my forehead, my face into my eyes as I cry. I say~ My dear Beloved Bridegroom this blood, your blood is forever for me. Even so these tears I cry, they are for you, forever only for you, my Jesus.

And so it is, God bottles the tears of the Saints. The tears of the Bride of Jesus even as these tears are well mixed, forever mixed with the precious blood of our Jesus. Bottled & Sealed with Love.

Psalms 56:8
Jesus is the Word made flesh. Jesus is love manifest.

Charles W. Warner

(Watcher on the Wall)

You are a Watcher on the wall. Call forth the glory of God. God lives here in our hearts~ God abides here in the atmosphere.

As a Son/Daughter of God,
As an Ambassador of the Kingdom of God
As a Watcher on the wall, call out, sing out, and celebrate Jesus!

As a Prophet of God, hear God's voice, hear God's heartbeat and repeat it back to hungry hearts. Hearts are hungry and only Jesus can satisfy a hungry heart.

Saddle up your horses, we have a trail to blaze.

You are a torch bearer, a fire starter, a water walker, a trail blazer! Fan the flame! Set the sea on fire! Rivers of flame! A human heart is as dry straw and Holy Ghost is a living blazing Wild Fire!!! We are calling Wild Fire!!!! Set hearts on fire, set this world ablaze as only you can do!!! My heart is a live wire and Holy Ghost is the Fire!

"I for one, as a 'Watchman on the Wall', cry out ... We need Jesus in this world like never before. Yes it's dark and getting darker, but with God I will not fall down and die to this greatest of callings! I stand! I go forth to proclaim the Good News, to raise the dead and heal the sick, to comfort, to testify, to love!

All Consuming Fire, consume all of me~ Refiners Fire refine me for your glory~ Take me as I am, make me ever new~ All I want to be is ever more like you, ever more in love with you my Lord~ my Love~ My Adonai.

God says of this Harvest of Nations, of cities, of souls- I will not relent I will burn hotter~ deeper~ higher- This Holy Ghost Revolution will usher in the return of the King of Glory's salvation story! Of this King and His Kingdom there shall be no end! The glory of King Jesus shall cover the earth as the water covers the sea!

~Join the Holy Ghost Revolution~ Say yes to Jesus & live~ Holy Ghost~ Baptism Of Fire!!!

Dear God take me with you.
Where you go I go.
Where you stay I stay.

Charles W. Warner

(D.N.A.)

God told me, to know that I have Kids and Grand Babies and I said yes, but they're not my kids biologically, God then walked me over to a corner and tapped me on the head and the heart and said" they are your Grand Babies spirit, soul, body for I make all things new. Adonai blood runs through our veins. Every strand of our DNA spells".

J E S U S

Jesus is the Vine we are the branches
We are planted in good soil
We are bearing good fruit
With good seeds after it's own kind
We drink deeply of this Living Water.

Charles W. Warner

(Judgement and Correction vs. Condemnation)

First thing always speak truth in love never speak bitter words in condemnation.

To those who say -

You can't judge me or that's your opinion not mine-
The Word of God brings judgment and correction

The Word of God is the absolute foundation of truth
whereby we build on this truth on this Rock of Ages.

"The Word of God is not a temporal opinion of man
The Word of God is the eternal truth of God"

We do not correct based on our opinions we proclaim the Holy
Bible, the Word of God.

The Word of God brings correction to the wise, to those who
choose to have eyes to see and ears to hear.

The Word of God brings judgment to the fool who choose to remain
in his sin, who choose to be the blind leading the blind.

Hebrews 4:12

*For the word of God is alive and active. Sharper than any
double-edged sword, it penetrates even to dividing soul
and spirit, joints and marrow; it judges the thoughts and
attitudes of the heart.*

*Speak truth in love. Yes truth can hurt for a season, for a
time but living a lie will always kill steal and destroy.*

John 10:10

*The thief cometh not, but for to steal, kill, and destroy: I
am come that they might have life, and that they might
have it more abundantly.*

John 14:6
*Jesus answered, "I am the way, the truth and the life. No
one comes to the Father except through me.*

Romans 8:1

There is therefore now no condemnation to them which are in Christ Jesus, who walk not after the flesh, but after the Spirit. So warn them who walk in error, in sin. Speak in truth, love and Godly wisdom while warmly welcoming correction from those who love you...

2nd Timothy 3:16 "All scripture is given by inspiration of God, and is profitable for doctrine, for reproof, for correction, for instruction in righteousness."

Proverbs 10:17 "People who accept discipline are on the pathway to life, but those who ignore correction will go astray."

Hebrews 12:11ISV "No discipline seems pleasant at the time, but painful. Later on, however, for those who have been trained by it, it produces a harvest of righteousness and peace."

P.S.

Fools say of the wise, "you are a hater!" That is your opinion, not mine! Translation: let me sin in peace, let me live my own life in a pool of lies and compromise. An opinion is a view or judgment formed about something, not necessarily based on fact or knowledge. Jesus is the Prince of peace. There is no peace, truth, wisdom or good without God.

"God is Not Mocked: for whatsoever a man sows that shall he also reap!" ~ Galatians 6:7

"FOOLS make a Mock at Sin..." ~ Proverbs 14:9 ~

"The Holy Bible is not a Book of tolerance towards sin and hate towards man. The Bible is the Book of Salvation, grace and true love.

Speak truth in love. A story- You better tell me the truth if I'm about to pick up a hot pan and you knew it, watching me pick it up and you say well I did not want to offend you, I did not want to judge you, I did not want to correct you! You need to learn on your own the hard way. If I warned you, you would think I'm a hater that it's simple my opinion, only God can judge you. Now I am here with a hurt hand you could of helped!? How much more should we help, warn those of Hell fire! The Human heart is as dry straw Holy Ghost is a wild Fire bringing Living Water to those who thirst, the Bread of Life to those who are hungry. We all need Jesus. John 3:16

Charles W Warner

(Go Light The World)

The way of starting revival is kindling the fire within oneself....igniting it to such a passionate burning desire for Him that it ignites those around you.

When Believers shine, it is because the Glory of the Lord is revealed. Shine brightly!

Arise, shine, for your light has come, and the glory of the LORD has risen upon you. Isaiah 60:1†

Do all things without grumbling or disputing, 15 that you may be blameless and innocent, children of God without blemish in the midst of a crooked and twisted generation, among whom you shine as lights in the world, Philippians 2:14-15 †

And those who are wise shall shine like the brightness of the sky above; and those who turn many to righteousness, like the stars forever and ever. Daniel 12:3 †

In the same way, let your light shine before others, so that they may see your good works and give glory to your Father who is in heaven. Matthew 5:16 †

For God, who said, "Let light shine out of darkness," has shone in our hearts to give the light of the knowledge of the glory of God in the face of Jesus Christ. 2 Corinthians 4:6 †

Again Jesus spoke to them, saying, "I am the light of the world. Whoever follows me will not walk in darkness, but will have the light of life." John 8:12 †

Charles W.Warner

(This Tree)

This tree is planted in good soil to worship God.
To sing forth the joy of Jesus.
To dance in the wind of the Holy Ghost.

I plant trees, I lay rocks for just this cause.

Rocks and trees don't cry out in my place, but they do cry out loud
and clear when I;

Pray, proclaim, prophesy. Sing forth God's glory and live out His love. Draw hearts home to Jesus, led and fed by the wind and fire of Holy Ghost. God thy Kingdom come to earth as it is in Heaven.

It's time even as eternity over takes time for the dropping of acorns, the planting of seeds.

"The Garden and the Kingdom"

Whirlwind planting of the seeds.
The Garden and the Kingdom.
The natural and the supernatural.

Isaiah 44: 3-4

Amos 9: 13

Charles W. Warner

(The Song Of The Sea)

This little girl
tells her little brother
this story
this song of the sea.

God is in Heaven.
God is in the clouds.
God is in our hearts.

God is in the heavens.
God is in the wind & sea.
God is in you and me.

God of the birds.
God of the flower.
God is with us every hour.

God of the sun.
God of the sand.
God holds us in His hand.

Charles W. Warner

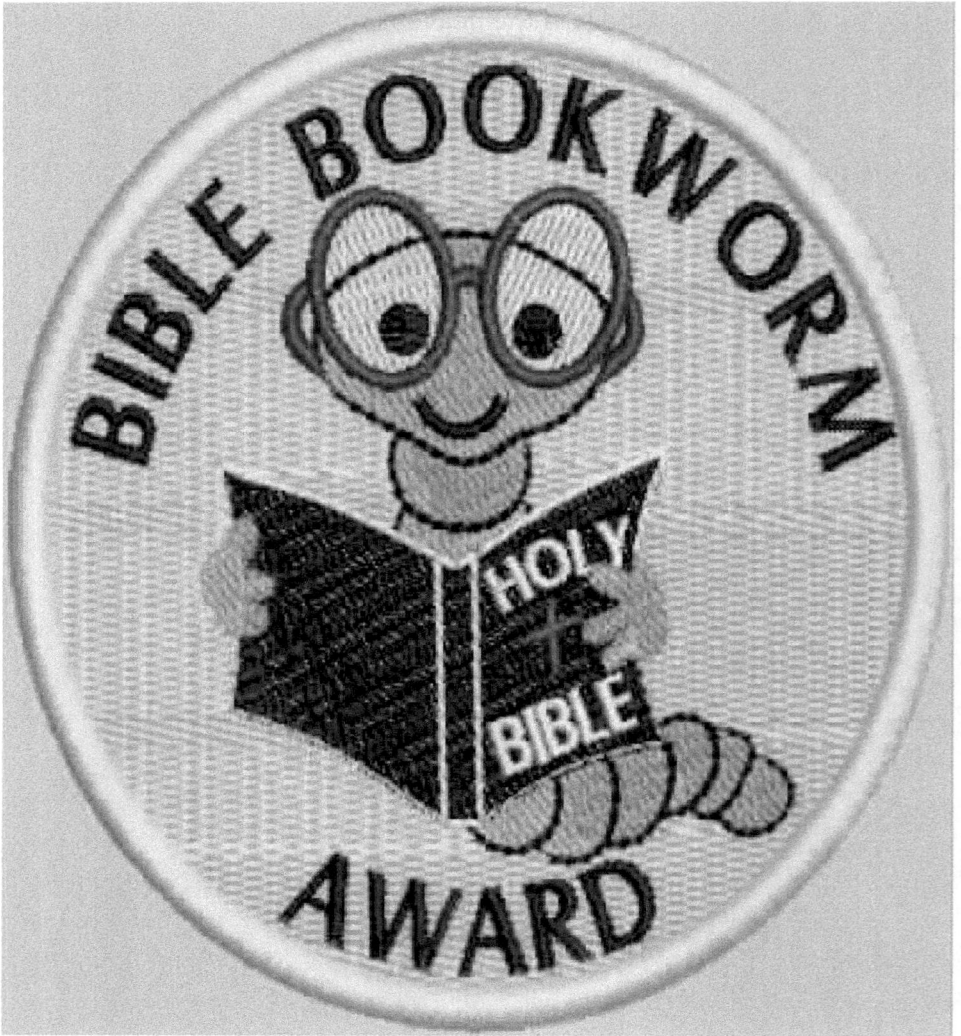

(WE ARE ONE)

~This is a vision, a true account of my time with Jesus~

If you have a vision write it done & make it clear.

I was at my desk writing and then in a flash in a blink of an eye I was in a large bright room with books,

I was at a desk, then all of a sudden Jesus came to me wrapped His arms around me, in silence He spoke to me, with no audible words yet with the clearest, deepest of meaning, for we are one.

I know my Shepherds voice He speaks to me. Every fiber of my being hears His call, hear His heart.
Jesus says Charles you are welcome here you are needed here, this house, this library was built for you to draw wisdom, knowledge and truth. Seek & you shall find. Charles you and I are one and we are one with the library. Then I said- So Jesus is this your way of saying we are book worms? Jesus pause smile and then laugh saying yes we are book worms! He pause again and says Charles you are funny! I say you should know you created me! Jesus says-
Yes indeed I did lol

We are one, we are one, I say it with Him we are one, we are one. Then I'm back on earth at my desk. I cry out noooooooooooo!!! I want to go back, I need to go back! Please I'm not done we are one! I need you Jesus to stay with me, don't leave me! Then the air is charged, there is living light, love is all around. There standing before me is my Lord Jesus He throws His arms around me embracing me in a big bear hug! He says we are one I say it with Him we are one. For a time this is what we say for how long I do not know.

Then Jesus says I AM always with you
I will never leave you & He takes me in His arms saying
We are one we are one we are one I again say it with Him
We are one, we are one, we are one
Jesus takes me in His arms, In His heart, we are one
In this I know how long we say this not just for a time for all time
and eternity
for this is our ~HEART BEAT~ We are one.
I am my Beloved and He is mine.
~~~WE ARE ONE~~~

Charles W. Warner

(That's How I Roll)

I am a blood bought, sanctified, free, and molded by the Potters hand, born again Christian that is a geek for God!!! That's how I roll!

To follow many ways to God is to follow the spirit of Anti-Christ. To thine own self be true is the calling card to self-glory, to self-distortion, to self-destruction. Trust in God lean not onto they own understanding...

I'm following God based on my situations and feelings or I'm following God by faith, believing God's promises, seeking God heart to heart, being lead & fed by the Holy Ghost. ~I feed on the fire of Holy Ghost~

Charles W. Warner

(This Blood)

This blood is for you.
My blood is for you.
My love is for you.

Come just as you are~ broken and blind in a cold, dark world.

Come just as you are~ I will comfort and keep you.

Come just as you are~ I am your Savior, your Redeemer and Friend.

Come just as you are~ Rest here at the foot of the cross, all is not lost.

Fall into my arms my love. I will carry you and care for you forever more.

Fall into the Arms of Love and live.

"JESUS the name above all names"

Charles W. Warner

I see you there hanging on a tree.
You bled and then you died and then you rose again for me.
Now you are sitting on your heavenly throne.
Soon we will be coming home.
You're beautiful, you're beautiful.

When we arrive at eternity's shore,
where death is just a memory and tears are no more.
We'll enter in as the wedding bells ring.
Your bride will come together and we'll sing,
"You're beautiful, You're beautiful, You're beautiful."

(The Cross)

God's Creation My Collection

I have this sea shell collection and I saw there was a shell missing. I was like, how sad, I have a missing sea shell it's incomplete ...

Till one day I saw this old, rusty, rugged cross. I added the cross and now, with the cross, it's better than new!

So it is with our lives. Do you have a piece missing?
Are you lonely, scared, bored, confused, tired, and sad?
Do you have anything/everything this world can offer
yet you know~ there must be more?

Please ask Jesus into your life, your heart.
Jesus makes all things new, better than new.

I needed to add this cross to my collection
just like I needed to ask Jesus into my life, my heart
as Savior & Lord. In Jesus I live, move and have my being. Jesus is
my life, my love, my song, my everything. Jesus is my All in All.

Life without Jesus is incomplete. Only Jesus can satisfy a hungry heart
Life without Jesus is like a broken pencil it has no point.

Acts 17:28   For in him we live and move and have our being.' As some of your own poets have said, 'We are his offspring.

Charles W. Warner

(Flower Garden of Life)

In our garden, flowers take time to grow.
In our garden, the sun will shine.
In our garden, the rain will fall.
In our garden weeds will try to grow, but no, for we love our little garden.
Yes, in our garden, flowers take time to grow. Yet it's well worth ever second for in our little stone garden Jesus is our Rock.

"Love grows deep roots & sweet fruits"

Charles W. Warner

*"And God said, "Behold, **I have given you every plant yielding seed which is upon the face of all the earth**, and every tree with seed in its fruit; you shall have them for food."*
—*Genesis 1:29 (RSV)* -

(Baby Prayer)

Dear Daddy

Father God, through Jesus, you are my dear Daddy. In Jesus we are one.

Dear Daddy mold me and make me ever new.

Whisper to my mind your glory unfold.

Whisper to my heart love stories untold.

May I shine bright with your glory and live out your love.

May my newly created heart ever beat as a love song, totally devoted to my beloved Daddy.

May my developing lungs breathe in deep the breath of life, for you are the air I breathe.

My little nose and tiny toes are formed and fashioned by my Master Potter.

I have my Fathers eyes and my Daddy's heart, for I am His and He is

forever mine.
Dear Daddy I am not yet born, yet I want you to know....
Dear Daddy you are my world, you are my song.
May I always dance with my Dear Daddy, tiny toes and all
signed, Beloved

Charles W. Warner

life isn't about
waiting for the
storm to pass...
it's about
learning to
dance in the rain

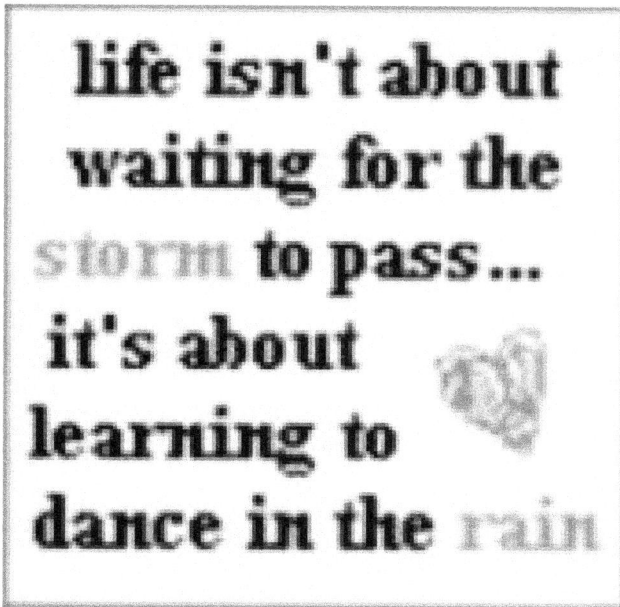

(The Storm and The Rock)

There is a parting going on of those who play church those who play in the sand out of manmade religion and those who build on the Rock of Ages ~JESUS~ those who are the Church, the Bride based on love, trust and a living growing, over flowing relationship with Jesus. This is not based on performance meaning we can't earn Salvation/redemption it's a free gift called grace this is based 100% on Jesus our soul provider our all in all.

There is a great storm at sea the storm has a rip tide pulling any who gets in the sea
Many choose to foolishly play in the sea at their own parole
Many chose to stay & build in the shifting, sinking sand-
& there by their lives are washed away into the deep black sea

There is a hillside where the wise run and are saved

Build your house your home on this holy hill
Build your house your home on "The Rock Of Ages"

On this Rock there is built The Church
God is coming as living lighting
To rock & rattle the church
To hit the church as living lighting
To knock off the barnacles

God is here as Living Lighting
God is here as an All-consuming Fire
God is here as a Refiners Fire

God is here to consume the church
To set the church on fire
To burn away the lethargy & lukewarm
God is here to awaken the dead & dyeing, to awaken the frozen
chosen.

The lost are crying out is this sea all there is?
Is this life just a few short years and then we die to be known no
more?
Are we nothing but sand driven by the raging winds?
Whoever you are wherever you are arise & run to the Rock
Jesus is The Rock, a sure and steady foundation
Run to The Rock of your Salvation
Fall on This Rock & He will comfort you
He will lift you up. Jesus is the wind under your wings

~Rock of Ages~

Rock of Ages clefted for me let me hide myself in thee.
Lord God over shadow me with thy wing.
Lord you alone are my soul provider.
Lord you lift me up higher & higher for you are the wind

under my wings.

Can these dead dry bones live again? In Jesus yes we will live again
we shall shine-
brighter than ever.

Arise and shine! For your light has come; the glory of the LORD has risen upon you. For behold, the darkness shall cover the earth, and deep darkness the people; But the Lord shall arise over you, and His glory shall be seen upon you. The Gentiles shall come to your light, and kings to the brightness of your rising. Isaiah 60:1-3.

The work of the gospel the Good News is not to close with a lesser display of the Holy Spirit's power then marked it's beginning.

Awake, the wave of The Holy Spirit is here. Run to the Rock and live.

A holy judgement is soon to befall us. Judgement is coming as a huge tidal wave of the Holy Spirit to awaken the sleeping church, to awaken the sleeping Bride of Jesus. The Bride must stop hiding her head in the shifting, sinking sands of manmade religion. The Bride must awake to her calling she must now run to the rock The Rock of Ages and build her house there not Just visit there! Jesus is my Savior not my religion.

This tidal wave is here and is coming in deeper, higher, faster it is a flood of the Blood of Jesus.
This wave is Holy Wild Fire, uncontrollable, unstoppable, ever growing.
This wave is
The Covenant Blood,
Holy Wild Fire,
Grace, Glory.

This wave is the very presence of God with us.

Shaking and Awakening~

I see a might Lion roaring. I see a mighty wave racing across the land. I see a mighty tidal wave of the blood of the Lamb of God crashing into the church breaking out of the four walls of the church. Outgrow over flow- Open the flood gates of heaven Let it rain with the love of the Lord, let it rain more and more let it pour wind, rain and fire!! Let it flood with the blood of Jesus!!!

The Glory of God shall cover the earth as the waters cover the sea. And of my Kingdom there shall be no end.

I said it before & I will say it again-
This world is shifting, sinking sand... Cry out to Jesus & live... In a world of shifting sinking sand Jesus and only Jesus is the Rock of Ages. This world is The Titanic. Jesus is The Ark.
Charles W. Warner

There is joy in knowing
a strong woman
who is confident and proud
without being unkind.

There is joy in knowing
a beautiful woman
who brings forth
that beauty in others...

(CAN WOMEN PREACH?)

I was asked- "Charlie you're a man! Why are you standing up for Women's rights?" Wow! After that, God with me, I shall stand for women's rights all the more! This sets me on fire, a holy fire, to preach, teach God's eternal truth. Not man's temporary traditions. I will take after Jesus example and stand for women's rights! I'm proud to be a man standing for women's rights!!!

Galatians 3:28 There is neither bond nor free, there is neither male nor female: for we are all one in Christ Jesus.

Gal 4:7 Wherefore thou art no more a servant, but a son; and if a son, then an heir of God though Christ.

We are Sons of God and The Bride of Jesus. Jesus commissioned us all to The Great Commission not just men. Matthew 28:16-20

If women are to stay home washing dishes while the men only hear from Jesus and tell the Gospel/preach then why is it that Mary Magdalene was the first one to see Jesus alive and to tell the Gospel to preach the Good News that Jesus lives?!!! Jesus told Mary to go tell his disciples that he is alive. Yes Mary was the first one to tell, to preach the gospel, the good-news that Jesus lives!

What about the woman who anointed Jesus with tears & costly perfume & dried his feet with her hair? She was preaching the gospel, the good-news. She was a silent witness yet she spoke so loud and clear.

Why did Jesus tell the woman at the well to go tell her Family that Jesus is here with us? Jesus the promised Messiah if women can't preach? Also the disciples wondered why Jesus was even talking to a woman, a Gentile a non-Jew. Tradition was the Gospel was to be preached only to the Jews, yet Jesus came for all people.

Joel 2:28 And it shall come to pass afterward, that I will pour out my spirit upon all flesh; and your sons and your <u>daughters shall prophesy</u>, your old men shall dream dreams, your young men shall see visions:

Is 60:1 Arise, shine; For your light has come! And the glory of the Lord is risen upon you.

Is 61:1 The Spirit of the Lord God is upon me; because the Lord hath anointed me to preach good tidings unto the meek; he hath sent me to bind up the brokenhearted, to proclaim liberty to the captives, and the opening of the prison to them that are bound;

Is 55:11 So shall my word be that goeth forth out of my mouth: it shall not return unto me void, but it shall accomplish that which I please, and it shall prosper in the thing whereto I sent it.

Matt 28: 18-20 And Jesus came and spake unto them, saying, all power is given unto me in heaven and in earth.

19 Go ye therefore, and teach all nations, baptizing them in the name of the Father, and of the Son, and of the Holy Ghost:

20 Teaching them to observe all things whatsoever I have commanded you: and, lo, I am with you always, even unto the end of the world. Amen.

A person can be preaching from the Bible and be preaching nothing but dead works and manmade religion. You don't have to wear a robe or a veil. You don't have to be a man to preach, you can be a man, woman, boy or girl. We preach with our actions & our words, we preach out loud and we live the Good News as a silent witness, letting God speak through us. Here is something else. We don't have to stand in the limelight on Sunday night behind a pulpit to preach.

When Jesus returns when that trumpet blows, nothing will matter. Only the souls we reached. Oh how I love Jesus, because He first loved me. So I will speak, write, proclaim, prophesy and preach.

Men, women, boys and girls live out love. Lift up Jesus, and if Jesus be lifted up, Jesus will draw all people to Himself.

John 12:32 And I, if I am lifted up from the earth, I will draw everyone unto myself."

Lift high the name of JESUS with me, far above any name, and let the manmade Jesus crumble to the ground and blow away in the Holy Ghost Wind!

Women are told to not wear paints, then told to cover their face while removing makeup. Women are told they must not preach, to keep silent, to keep order in the church. There also was a time where slaves were told to obey their masters.

There is freedom in the Holy Ghost. If you want to remain in slavery to the old letter of the law, traditions and customs, go ahead. But it's better to live by grace, from glory to glory in fellowship with God. I will live under the eternal blood covenant of Jesus. Not some temporary tradition of man's laws.

P.S. Women were told to remain silent in church, as in, if they had questions ask/(pray) their husbands at home. It was also said if you are hungry eat at home, don't come to church to eat the communion as your lunch.

P.S. Preaching isn't even about titles! When the Holy Ghost calls a Sister, a woman of God to stand up and preach words of wisdom please don't try to set her down! Lol
Charles W.Warner (pictured niece Kayla McDermott and Pastor Pam Harding)

(Be Still)

Silence is not a sin- Be still and know that God is God. This means turn off your cell phone, turn off your lights and turn on your heart to hearing from God. On the other side of the coin, on a busy Monday we can sing and hear from God. Whistle while you work & praise God all day long.

When God gives us a word, we need to speak, to talk, to share, to shine. Other times, we simply need to walk away, and lay our little heads on our big pillows and let God do what he does best. Be still and know I Am God.

"The mouth speaks loud some louder than others but not as loud as the heart"

"Speak truth live love"

Psalm 46:10. "Be still, and know that I am God; I will be exalted among the nations, I will be exalted in the earth. NLT. Proverbs 10:19. Don't talk too much for it causes sin. Be sensible and turn off the flow. Proverbs 18:21 Death and life are in the power of the tongue: and they that love it shall eat the fruit thereof.

Charles W. Warner

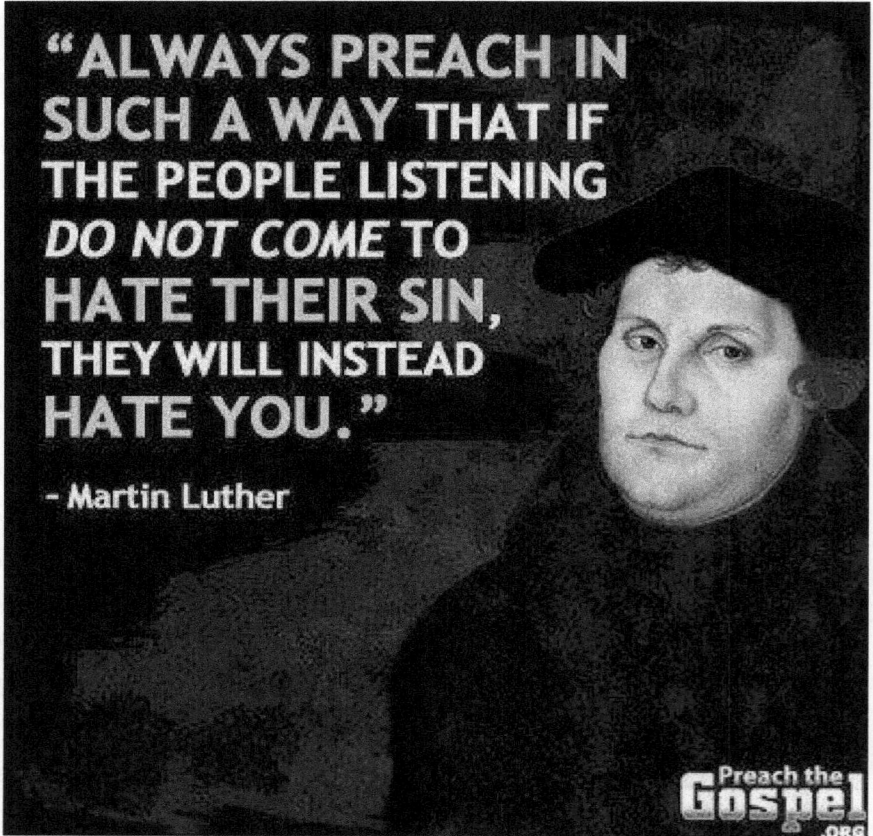

"ALWAYS PREACH IN SUCH A WAY THAT IF THE PEOPLE LISTENING *DO NOT COME TO* HATE THEIR SIN, THEY WILL INSTEAD HATE YOU."

- Martin Luther

Preach the **Gospel** .ORG

(Be Bold)

Never water down the Gospel to appease people. The Good News is meant to bring conviction onto repentance. Lukewarm is pacified religion! Let's be all the more on fire with a living relationship with God!!!"

Charles W. Warner

(Prayer- Deep Speaking Onto Deep)

Last year I was going to go to IHOP, (prayer not pancakes), with my friend. A friend who is a best friend of Misty Edwards.

Well it never happened. I forgot why, but we did not go. So I was a bit sad. I so wanted to sing with Misty, to sing to our Jesus and worship God with my peeps. We were going to go to the Mall and park, go out for ice cream, and go to IHOP (pancakes). That was the week of the 4th of July. We were going to watch the fireworks and celebrate.

So a while after this I had a vision~ I was praying over Misty Edwards, praying in agreement, an intercessory prayer, a travelling prayer, a prophetic prayer in English and spoken in tongues of the Holy Ghost. After praying I opened my eyes and Misty has misty eyes, crying in a pool of tears, shaking on her knees with hands raised. Praying heart to heart from God's heart.

I awoke from the vision and thought nice that was a sweet day dream. God stopped me and said "NO it was not a simple day dream! It was a prayer spirit to spirit, heart to heart orchestrated by Holy Spirit. This was an open vision, a prayer portal, a teleportation in the Holy Ghost. God says~ So Charlie you see you got to visit your Sister Misty after all. Heart to heart in the Holy Ghost!" I did not get to see fireworks in the natural, yet, Wow! There were fireworks in the Spirit and we celebrated Jesus.

Know who you are in me
Know who I am in you
For we, are One

(Deep)

How deep
How high
How wide
Is the love of God?

Endless
Limitless Love
Ever Abiding

Love lifted me
And Love
Calls me into the deep

For I am my Beloved and He is mine
Where He goes I go
Where He stays I stay

For we are one and so shall we ever be.

"Hear the song of love as it is played on the strings of your heart"

I don't want to live without love.
I am being formed and fashioned in love to be born of love. Take away the distractions and give me pure love, for I am loved by love. I am love, for love calls me by name. He calls me Beloved One, and I call Him, My Everything, My King of Glory. I am my beloved and He is mine.

I can live without many things love is not on that list.
Take the whole world but give me my Jesus

Charles W. Warner

(Let Us Unite)

Let us unite, let us lift high the banner of true love & lasting peace.

Let us unite, let us stand for something/someone greater than self, greater than selfishness and greed.

Let us unite, let us see the need of our fellow Brother and Sister.

Let us unite, let us see each other not based on the color of our skin or the size of our pocketbook, but on the cry of our hearts.

Let us unite, we all need to be loved, to be understood, we all need a hug sometimes.

Let us unite, lifting high the name of Jesus, and singing loud the song of "Love Lifted Me".

The human heart is hungry, and only Jesus satisfy the human heart. This world is cold, dark and lonely~ This world is shifting, sinking sand and only Jesus is the Rock of Ages. This world is the Titanic ~Jesus is the Ark.

You're my Brother, you're my Sister, so take me by the hand and we will work, live & love until Jesus comes.

Holy Ghost work here, live here, love here in our hearts.
Charles W. Warner

Jesus may you always be as a fire burning in our hearts. A Heavenly incense, God's gift to us.
People don't care how much you know until they know how much you care.

Charles W. Warner

(In the Arms of Love)

Jesus you are my freedom.
My passion .
My prize .
Jesus you are my Lord.
My life.
My love.
Jesus you are my one desire.
Jesus you are the fire.
that burns in my bones.

My heart sings because Jesus is my Savior. My heart burns because Jesus is my beloved and I am His. My heart is His Home and with Him will I ever abide. Jesus my one and only. ❤

"God cannot give us a happiness and peace apart from Himself, because it is not there. There is no such thing."

C. S. Lewis

Jesus without you, I'm like a fish without the sea. Where would I be? I'm like a bird without the sky. Lord without you I would surely die. I'm like a train without the rail, a sailboat without the sail, a carpenter without a nail.

Jesus I know you were a carpenter and you had your nails. Jesus you had your nails one in each hand and one in your feet. Jesus thank you for the cross where you died for the lost. Thank you Jesus that all things are new though you.

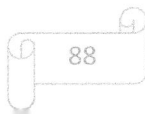

"Run to Jesus fall at His feet and he will lift you up. Beauty for ashes, strength for fear. Not all that glitters is gold. Sin can seem fun, glamorous and cool but sin is a cheap substitute for the real thing. Sin is a trap, a hook to drag you to Hell. Unless you're willing to walk there and bring others with you. Jesus is the real thing. He bled and died for you. Will you stand up and live for Him? Sin will call to you but it has nothing good to give. Only death and decay. Only lies.

"We live in God's presence."
"We trust in his promises, we rest in his love."

Charles W. Warner

(Wild Fire)

Arise and live, arise and dance, arise and sing, arise and shine for the glory of our Lord is here.

Holy Ghost blaze before us set us on fire.
Holy Ghost we are a live wire and you are the Fire.

Burn in me, burn in me, burn in me.
Watch me glow,
Watch we show forth your glory & live out your love.

Lord God, Dear Daddy you are the Fire that ever burns in these bones

Release the burning ones those with fire in their bones.

Dance, dance, dance, Dance in the fire, fan the flames.

My heart sings. My hands are holy. My feet are on fire. I will dance with Jesus in the desert and watch the desert bloom.

Here and now we prophecy, these dead and dry bones shall live. Shall live, sing, dance, praise and prophecy before her Messiah. Awake oh Zion. Behold thy King oh Israel. Awake hearts that hunger. Behold thy light has come. Victory sweet victory in Jesus.

Wild Fire burn in me. Over flow. Set this world on fire. God for your glory we dance. In you we live, move and have our being.

Isaiah 69:1 Arise, shine; for thy light is come, and the glory of the LORD is risen upon thee.

Charles W. Warner

Artist Jewell Jeffery

TRANSFORMED

INTO THE SAME IMAGE FROM GLORY TO GLORY

this is from the Lord who is the Spirit

2 Corinthians 3:18

Lord, make me a butterfly. Pleases give me wings. Dear God this life hasn't been easy. Filled with rejection, deception and many long nights. The tears have been plenty and the pain unrelieved. With these wings I will soar high, above all my pain and sadness. I will be beautiful on the outside for all to see, for I know now I am no beauty. My heart has been so broken, so abused and betrayed. The darkness engulfs me, the future I cannot see. Life is so uncertain dear God, much more than what it used to be. I'm desperate for you dear God. I cannot go on a moment more without you. I will not make it to see the morning light. Please hold me tight dear sweet, Jesus. In your arms I run, in your arms I hide. Safe and secure in your healing power and wonderful saving grace. Your strong ever-loving arms envelope me. I feel your grace and your mercy. You will never betray me nor break my heart. I need you so much. Thank you dear Jesus! You have rescued me, saved me from the prison of myself. In your light I will ever be. I know it may not be easy, there may still be some tears. But praise you dear Jesus, I won't do it alone. I now see so clearly what I could not see before. For you hold my tears and my heart. You alone are my salvation. You will break these chains of addiction and depression and fear. I do not need wings, I do not need to fly. I won't have to run from my problems. That has never worked out before. Instead I turn to you Jesus. In your precious blood I am free. Wiped clean and beautiful now, in my heart that only You can see. You know me by name, you love me anyway. I WILL soar with the eagles now for I am truly your butterfly.

Connie Warner

(New Birth)

As we rise from the ashes of our old lives we resurrect and break forth into the new!

I arise out of the ashes of the old.
I arise, beauty for ashes, strength for fear.
Tears of sorrow turned to tears of joy.

For Jesus is my joy and my strength,
"Jesus the Beautiful One".

I arise and shine, with healing in my wings.
I arise and shine, as a phoenix, as a fire.
I arise in power and authority to call forth the Kingdom of my God and King.

I arise to sing and dance in the glory of my King.
I live to call forth the Gospel, the Good News.

Hallelujah! Jesus is alive! Your chains have been broken. It is well, it is finished. Jesus has won. Fall at the feet of Jesus and know, the Way, the Truth, the Life, the Light of the world, and true love that your heart cries out for.

Jesus, my heart is full tonight as I come to you. There is peace in my spirit as I praise and worship You in all your magnificent glory. I bathe in your shadows and rays of light as I am engulfed in Your most holy fire. I am on fire with your Spirit tonight and I can feel you here with me as you whisper words to me. Some for myself and some to share. I will do as I am being lead to do. God has a lot for me, I receive your fire your heart's desire to burn in me Lord.

Charles and Connie Warner   Amy Rylander- Artwork

(My Rainbow)

I see this is God, as a Rainbow. A covenant, a promise and a provision. God is saying to the Church, the Bride" I Am with you. I am always with you. We are one in the Son." Let us run with our Rainbow. Let us go with dominion in our hands and fire in our feet, to every land. Taking back what is rightfully ours in Jesus. Let us ride this wave of glory, 'Salvation Story'.

This Rainbow is God with us. Taking back the land. From highest hill to lowest valley, God is taking back what is His. Taking by force! God will not quit or slow down. God will never relent! We as God's blood-bought sons and daughters, will run this race. We will take what is ours. We will not look back at yesterday. For this is a new day and hour. To usher in the soon return of the King of Glory, Jesus, our Lord and King.

In Jesus, we have every right and responsibility, to run with our precious Rainbow. God is with us. Holy Ghost is here, and with Jesus we win! It is finished! Let's take this land for Jesus. Let's lift His name high, and if He be lifted high, He will draw all onto Himself. Fire fall, wind blow, here we go with our Rainbow.

Charles W. Warner

Amy Rylander Art's photo.

(Anointed Pen)

Pick up your anointed pen given to you from God. You have a story to write. A song to sing. Write it down as only you can!

Draw forth your pen from the stone. For only you can draw forth and call forth your personal pen. Presented to you from God's heart to your heart. Draw forth your pen from the stone, draw forth your pen from the "Rock of Ages" and write.

You are called to be salt and light. A city on a hill. You are a mighty oak tree planted in good soil. Planted by rivers of water. Drink deep of this Living Water. Grow strong, deep roots in the "Rock of Ages". Multiply, bring forth good fruit with seeds after its own kind. Eat the Fruit of The Holy Spirit and reproduce most abundantly!

Multiply 30X 60X 100X 1000X fold.

How high, how deep, how wide is the love of God? Limitless, endless. Come and drink of this Living Water that shall never run dry. Take and eat of this Living Bread. Overflow!!!

Ask what you will. Pray, and I will answer you. Above and beyond

what you can hope, dream or imagine.

Ephesians 3:20-21. (20) Now unto him that is able to do exceeding abundantly above all that we ask or think, according to the power that worketh in us, (21) Unto him be glory in the church by Christ Jesus throughout all ages, world without end. Amen.

Charles W. Warner

(The Walk)

I saw myself in a dream.
In a dream I am walking down a park pathway. I come to an open park that is filled with people who seem to be forming some type of meeting or debate. A tall man in a fine silk suit with a matching feathered hat welcomes me saying,

"Welcome, good sir .We are gathered here to find God!
Billy Bob over there, presumes and assumes that he has the best method to hear from God, but nooooo no no no!
It's more like a math then a method!"

"You see, you have to be loud. Real loud and proud!!! You got to stand out behind the pulpit!!! Boy, you have to stand out in a crowd! You have to be head and shoulders above the next guy and let everybody know you're the King of the castle!!!

Little Billy Bob says you have to bow low, real low . To hide in the shadows and shallows, never deep.

Anonymously give and never receive. To fast and never feast, at the Lords Table.

To be a church mouse, not a mighty man of God.
To be a beggar in prayer, not a Son or not a Daughter.
To have an orphan spirit, always at want.
Never a King or a Queen.
Never to be known as The Beloved Bride of the King of Kings.
Not an heir or co-heir in the Kingdom of God.
Never a royal ambassador, commanding God's Word. Never proclaiming nor prophesying all God's promises are" yes and amen" in Jesus.
Not standing boldly before God, but falling to the fear of man.
You see I am strong in the power of my own might.
I know who I am. I do it my way! Not like little boy Billy Bob, hahaha!

So tell me do you know God, and what is your name boy!?"

Do I know God? By God's grace, yes I do know Him and love Him. If there is anything good about me blessed be God forever. God spells love JESUS and so do I. The only atonement between God and man is the perfect blood of Jesus. Jesus, and Jesus alone is the mediator between man and God. So put away your manmade religion of trying to reach God on your own merits. Fall at the foot of the cross. Fall at the feet of Jesus. Fall into the arms of love and live.

My past does not define me.
My past does not hold me.

Jesus, my Beloved one, defines me, holds me, and keeps me.
God, all I want to be is in your presence.

My name is child of the one true King! King of kings and Lord of Lords. The Lion and the Lamb of glory. That's my Jesus. I know who I am by knowing who He is. For when I am lost in His love then am I found in Him. I am my Beloved and He is mine. Jesus my Beloved. Now that's who I am. Who are you?

Romans 8:16-17

16 The Spirit itself beareth witness with our spirit, that we are the children of God:

17 And if children, then heirs; heirs of God, and joint-heirs with Christ

Isaiah 55:11
Jeremiah 29:11
Zechariah 4:6
John 3:16-21
John 14:6Romans 8: 38-39
Acts 2:17

Charles W. Warner

(A Walk With Jesus)

I am in Heaven with my walking stick. I say "Wow my walking stick is glowing!" People laugh and say, so are you. Jesus walks up to me with His walking stick and says "May I walk with you a mile or two or more?" I say" You may always walk with me. It will be a walk to remember." A long legged stork comes to my side and asks, "May I walk with you in this walk and talk?" I say "Sure, you're more than welcome here."

We walk down streets of pure gold. Streets that appear as pearl. A rainbow bridge. A bridge of flowers, out across the crystal sea that glistens and glows. Down and around the gardens of God. We see singing flowers. We see willow trees the size of mountains, humming and whistling in the wind.

We come to a peaceful pond and Hark, the stork, says," Come follow me, new birth." Jesus says," I make all things new. Rest in my care. All is well my Bride. Come follow me deeper and higher. There are no limits to my love. No shadow of turning from glory to glory."

Gabriel says," Even as I have spoken to Mary, the Mother of Jesus, now I speak to you. The Bride of The Great I Am, The Bride of Jesus. It is time to give birth to Destiny and her twin sister Creativity."

Throughout eternity past, Jesus always wanted, always knew that He was destined to have a Bride. A beautiful, creative Bride and you're it!!! Many, yet one Bride, of the one and only Jesus. Our Bridegroom, the King of glory and our Prince of Peace.

If there is any good report, if there is anything lovely about me, then blessed be God forever. Jesus makes my life beautiful. Jesus the beautiful one. This world and its ways are not my home. Yet Jesus you will forever be my joy, my Beloved One.

I dedicate these Worship, waking, dancing sticks to the one I love, (God) (Jesus) (Holy Ghost). Set these sticks on fire!!! Well you know what I mean. Holy fire, glory, make them shine to draw hearts home to Jesus! Portals and impartations of Shekinah glory. God's tangible sweet anointing burning as sweet incense.

So I was just talking to Jesus and I asked him," Jesus since you are the Carpenter, my Creator, my Redeemer, and BFF (Best Friend Forever). Would you please help me make walking sticks? We can talk about it over tea." He said "yes", plus He reminded me that I have tea that is ready now. Even as He is always ready, there for me, here with me.

Someday, Jesus may we go for a walk, haha, walking sticks and all?

Charles W. Warner

(Beloved One)

Do you want to know true love lasting love & eternal wisdom? Then fall into the arms of love, hold on to Jesus nail scared hand.

Is there anything good about me? Am I patient & kind? Love is patient & kind. If there is anything lovely about me it's because Jesus is the beautiful one.

Charles W. Warner

(Brothers)

Yes I am a Jesus freak. What kind of freak are you???

The longer I live, the more I learn, the more I know that I do not want to live without Jesus! The Good News is Jesus loves me. This is a cold, dark, scary world without Jesus. Thank God I have Jesus and thank God he has me.

Charles W. Warner

Listen!

The Lord's arm
is not too weak to
save you, nor His
ear too deaf to
hear you call.

Isaiah 59:1

(Listen)

When things get you down, let the Lord lift you up.
Just call out and He will be there.
When you feel alone, lost and afraid, He will comfort you.
The Lord loves you like no other. We love because He loved us first...

Isaiah 59:1

Ancient of Days~ God almighty is my Ancient of Days, my Daddy, my deliverer & redeemer. God is the lifter of my heart & hand. God is my strength, my power, my mighty high Tower, my Rock of ages that shall never be moved, my Living Water that shall never run dry.

"Jesus is my joy & my song all the day long"
"I am a live wire, Holy Ghost is the Fire"

Charles W. Warner

(For Me)

"Jesus wore a crown of thorns that we may wear a robe of righteousness. He became sin who knew no sin that we may become his righteousness. Love so amazing." 2 Corinthians 5:21

(My Beloved Rose)

Flowers of all kinds and colors are simple to plant. Hard to forget and easy to love. Flowers are gifts from God above.

I walk down a cobblestone trail to a city full of fragrant flowers.

I smell lovely lilacs, lilies and lemon drops.
I see hills of heather, large oak trees with a million leaves.

I enter a rose garden there. I find a rose called Love and another called Peace. I walk through the garden for an hour at least.

I walk over to see bee balm, bell flowers and big butterflies. I see butterfly bushes and big bright sunflowers. Over the way I see Black Eyed Susan and Red Eyed Jane.

I think to myself what a wonderful day.
Soon I see Angel Wings and amazing things. I see the Rose of Heaven, Jacob's Ladder and Solomon's Seal. I hear a buzz, it's a bumble bee in a Tulip tree.
I think to myself how can this be?
Flower after flower, hour after hour.

I have seen evergreens and scenes of hummingbirds in Foxgloves. I see Icebergs near Red Hot Pokers. I see Holiday Holly and Rose Molly.

I lay down, for I am tired and lazy. I fall asleep with the Swan River Daisy. I soon walk across a beautiful bridge of hanging baskets, full of Marigolds, Violets, Peonies and Poppies.

I see many homes and parks full of flowers and trees, lined with pink Magnolia's, Red Maples, green Boxwood's, and white Dogwoods.

I see international plants - Mexican Sunflowers, African Violets, Irish Iris, Russian Sage and many more.

The most beautiful flower I keep for last. For this is the story of eternal love and glory, (Redemption story).Behold I see the Rose of Sharon, the Lily of the Valley, the Beautiful One burns as thee, all-consuming Fire, thee refiners fire. Sweet incense fills the air, fills my lungs, and fills my heart to overflow. Jesus' eyes are so warm, His smile so bright. Jesus my Beloved heart's delight.

Warmly and tenderly the Lord of glory, the Prince of peace calls me. Draws me to his open arms, to His heart. Yes, even now I hear Jesus call,"All is well my dove, my dear, for I hold you in my heart. Rest, all is well."

Jesus you are my joy.
Jesus you will always be my Flower, my Rose that grows, overflows from my heart.

Jesus is my all in all always.

Amen.

J E S U S

What a beautiful name

Charles W Warner.

(Destiny)

I see a barren, orange desert land that stretches as far as the eye can see. A flat land barren and of clay, devoid of vegetation except for a few cacti and burr bushes. Above and all around me the sky is the color and consistency of turmoil, ever increasing in size and motion. It expands into everywhere and nowhere. The clouds are ominous and dark. Shades of black and grey, vivid charcoal pillows fighting unseen evils. All colors vivid and looming large. A wide open battlefield, churning and choppy. Swollen with armies of angel warriors against the enemy and the darkness for our souls. The hidden sins and the demons we, and mainly my love fights. For he must battle these forces. The angels are strong and mighty. The size and legions of which I have never seen before. They are engulfed in the stormy clouds and I only catch glimpses of the many warrior angels as this battle for my loved one rages. So overwhelmingly large and beyond my understanding is this war for him to overcome. The spiritual warfare goes on, the clouds as thick, turbulent storm clouds.

Suddenly there begins a churning in the middle as if stirred by a large unseen hand stirring until the clouds are becoming smoother. The sky begins to lighten up and the clouds are not as threatening or as dark. The strength and magnificence of it all leave me in awe of my God and His amazing love for us. That He would send His angels to battle for us. He is showing us His purpose and love and soon the war is over and the saints have prevailed. Heaven opens and as the war weary warriors rejoice and return, it begins to rain. Strong, heavenly rain.

Water also pours down from where the angels fought as in a waterfall into the barren land. Not a usual rain, but one of milk and honey drenching us and this land. You, Charles, lift up your hands and you are soaking wet thoroughly through your clothes and self with the redemption of the triumph over your struggles. They are gone. We are whole in ourselves as individuals and we have been made one. You are dressed in the shirt and vest for our wedding. I am in my gown. The clothes turn to white and we glow, then return to the previous colors.

Soon all is settled and we see the land is no longer barren, but green, with grass and the water has become a stream. An abundant prairie full of life and light. Grasses grow taller and fuller as I watch, and soon tiny white flowers appear next to the extra tall grasses near the waters. Through the clear stream I can see stones in and around the water bed. I see a turtle sunning on one. There are now frogs and fish in what is rapidly becoming a river before my eyes. It looks like a beautiful green meadow now, and as I watch I see trees in the distance, butterflies and suggestions of a forest and a small house and homestead appear.

Now I see into the house and you (Charles) are seated in a large chair. All the furniture in the house is large, solid, dark wood and strong, well-made furniture. There is a large stone fireplace in use with a heavy mantle shelf, beautiful and strong. It is holding many pictures and solid old books. The house has many huge and solid bookcases filled with books. You are sitting in the chair among these things holding a very large pen God has given you. Not a modern pen but a black shiny old fashioned one, of the type that you dip into ink with a quill.

At this time you are told by God that "Now that you have truly overcome, you should write it. (About your secrets and how they could have destroyed you, but you and the angels have truly fought and overcome. Now you need to write about it *all*. Not just a little but your whole story...biography. .your true and LONG story complete with struggles and victories. Your book will help many others and God wants to use you for this.)

You and I have other talents we will use but none as powerful as where you were but are now delivered and are there no more. Your story and your writings. Your battle to overcome it will be our purpose for now. I will be by your side and through it all with you as your wife. Battles and victories. God has put us together as a team and you are the head and I will follow and be by your side, your partner. It is to be our mission together. God wants us to live by His word and follow the lead for marriage He has given us. You are the mighty lion of our marriage and the leader and we will obey God's words for ourselves and our marriage and love that He is blessing us with. Mighty sweet victory. Isaiah 43: 18-21

Connie Warner

(Embrace The Butterfly)

"Resurrection power"

On my own I am weak and wanting.
On my own I am lost and lonely.
On my own I feed on dust and dirt.
On my own I am spotted and speckled.

Good News! I am not on my own! I am not my own! Love lifted me!

On my own I am dust in the wind. Yet with God, I am clay in the hands of, "The Master Potter."

On my own I am a bug. A caterpillar feeding on dust and dirt. Feeding on the things this world has to offer. Feeding on trash in the picking and pecking order.

I am God's butterfly born anew, born again.
I am saved, I am redeemed. Love lifted me!
I am a butterfly. Free to fly, free to soar in the wind of Holy Spirit.
This butterfly is a live wire. I feed on the fire of Holy Ghost!
I hide myself in the cleft of the Rock, under the shadow of His wing
will I abide. I will fly higher than an eagle, for God is the wind beneath my wings.

Embrace the Butterfly.
This is a season to soar.
This is a season of new birthing's.
Breathe in glory, breathe out fire.
Spring forth with new songs.

I pick up my pen and write.

Jesus' Bride is being called to cry out the songs of the redeemed.
I will cry out. I will write out as God's Heart Scribe anointed words.

What I love about writing for God is; that what I write is sealed with His heart. To last beyond time into eternity. To celebrate Jesus now, and in that great forevermore. God is the Author and I am the co-author.

(My Redeemer Lives)

Behold our testimony. Our tears are to testify of God's great love.

Arise my love, the grave no longer has a hold on you. I have a hold on you, for I hold you in my hand and keep you in my heart.

God, I arise! Beauty for ashes, strength for fear. Tears of sorrow turned into tears of joy, "Jesus is my joy."

I will not lay back and die. In Jesus I fly high. Higher and higher God's heart's desire. Set this butterfly on fire. God is with me. We are one. So I fly, setting hearts on fire, to the joy of Jesus.

In Jesus we are all part of the body. We are many, yet one Bride. We serve as we are gifted, with our talents and time.

"Celebrate Jesus and love one another"

God says of this Harvest of souls," I will not relent. I will burn hotter, deeper, and higher. This Holy Ghost Revolution will usher in the return of the King of glory: salvation story. Of this King and His Kingdom there shall be no end. The glory of King Jesus shall cover the earth as the water covers the sea!

Charles W. Warner

(Day and Night)

Day and night.

Night and day.

Let incense arise.

I breathe in fire.
I breathe out incense.

Lord God I live to lift you up.
Lord God you are the air I breathe.
Lord God you are the fire that burns in my bones.

Charles W. Warner

(The Church)

Church is not just four walls, a carpet and a steeple. We are The Church, all God's people.

The Church house is a hospital, a boot camp, a place to gather to celebrate Jesus and love one another.

We as The Church need time together. We are the Body of Christ, a forever family bought by the blood of Jesus. A church building should be full of warmth and love, not dead bricks and cold hearts, so let us gather together to speak life and live out love.

Holy Ghost, you are most welcome, most needed in our hearts, our homes, and our church. God may we always see that grace is spelled J.E.S.U.S. God you are our All in All, in all places at all times.

I am a member of Faith Center.
I am a member of the household of faith.
I am a believer, a beloved of Jesus.
I am alive and active in the Kingdom of God.
I am led and fed by Holy Spirit.
I am led in all truth, all righteousness, and all wisdom.
I am using my gifts, my talents, and my time.
I live, I love, because God so loved me.

We are living stones,
we are washed by the Word of God,
washed by the Blood of Jesus.
We are alive and led by Holy Ghost.

We are living stones in the hands of a living God. In the hands of our God most high.

I stand in faith in God that my church, our church, Faith Center is highly favored & most blessed.

This church, Faith Center, counting the new building,
is built on good soil
is built on solid ground
is built on a good foundation
is built on The Rock of Ages.

This house shall prosper in all her ways.
This house is a House of Prayer, a Home of Love.
This house is built for the habitation of Holy Spirit.
This house is Holy & dedicated wholly to God.

We are Sons and Daughters of God.
We are the Bride of the Lamb of God (Jesus).
We are highly favored & most blessed to glorify our God.
We are a people, a church, and a house on a hill.
We will shine, we will glow.
We will show forth your glory and live out your love.
We shall be all and accomplish all to the glory of God.
For I am my Beloved & He is mine.

The Vision is simple.

People will: Come to hear, hear to learn,
learn to serve, serve to build God's Kingdom.

I sow my finances in the Kingdom of God. Every penny produces for God and for me.

The Gospel is preached in all the world. Lives are set free and the Kingdom of Satan is stopped.

It produces for me, "good measure, pressed down, shaken together and running over"

I count it as done in the name of Jesus

Charles W. Warner

(The Greatest Gift)

God speaks though his Word, the Holy Bible.
God speaks to our hearts in a still small voice.
God speaks though the winds and fire.
God speaks His heart's desire.

God speaks through people and angels.

God speaks in signs and wonders, dreams and visions.
God speaks through rocks, donkeys and the belly of a whale. God speaks as He sees fit, God knows better than I.
So speak Lord thy servant is listening.

Eyes to see and ears to hear.

I once heard a story of aliens coming to Earth landing in a UFO. An alien had a large book with the cure for cancer, the cure for all sickness and inventions of all kinds, to better the human race. The alien presented the book as a gift. How be it, a person was scared and shot an alien. So the aliens took the book back and said the human race is not ready for what is in the pages of their book and will return when we are ready. I thought, wow, if we only had that book now.

Yet there is good news. We have a book that is far better, priceless, filled with eternal promises. We have The Book, The Holy Bible. The Holy Bible is given to us from the heart of God, for God so loved.

The Bible story-
is the story of history, His- Story, Jesus story

The Bible story-
is the story of Jesus and His beloved Bride

Charlie W. Warner

(Unshackled)

We have all been incarcerated, in chains, in prison.
What prison did I come from?
I came from the prison of self-incarceration.
In bondage to sin believing lies
Jesus saved me from me!
Jesus is!
The Way vs. Lost
The Truth vs. Lies
The Life vs. Death
The Light of the World vs. Darkness
The Love of My Life vs. Chaos and Confusion

This world is shifting, sinking sand. Only Jesus is the Solid 'Rock of Ages' that shall not be moved.

This world is the Titanic.
Jesus is the Ark.

"Take the whole world but give me my Jesus."
Charles W. Warner

(Holy Fire)

I give the Word of God first place in my life.
I set my affection on God's Word.
I agree and submit to do whatever I see in God's Word.
I will obey God's Word over circumstances, people and Satan.

God's Word will produce for me, as far as I'm willing to commit to it.

Charles W. Warner

(Living Bible)

The Holy Bible is not a religious book.
Religion is man trying to reach a god of his own making by works, by
his own means and abilities, by his own traditions and customs.
The Bible is the story of grace, the redemption story
God so loved that he reached down to man.
(John 3:16)

The Holy Bible is a book of history, (His - Story). Jesus story.
The Bible is a book. The Book of prophecy and poetry.
The Holy Bible is the Gospel. The good news of Jesus.
The Holy Bible is the Book of God's promises to believe, to receive,
to proclaim, to live out loud.
Charles W. Warner

(My Holy Bible)

The Bible is the only Book you can read where the Author of the Book is always with you.

Be baptized in fire, The Shekinah Glory of God.

Live out love. Limitless and forever Agape Love.

Read the Word of God. The Rhema Word of God.

The Word of God and God of the Word is with me, so I do exploits in Jesus name. *Isaiah 61 John 14: 12-14*

When I say I am an author, I am in no way saying don't read your Bible. I am not competing with the Holy Bible. I write to lift up Jesus, to encourage you to read and study your Bible. In writing my books God is the Author I am the co-author.

The Holy Bible is not a book of shades of gray.
The Holy Bible is God's Book of absolute truth.
The Holy Bible is not open for man's interpretation of truth. It says what it says and it means what it means.."The truth is the truth regardless if you believe or not."

Charles W. Warner

(Start A Fire In Me)

Rain on me Jesus like an all might flood! A wave of water, a title wave of glory! Yes start a fire in me, for we all need you Jesus! This fire will never die will not relent.... This fire will consume hearts! This fire will consume Nations! Fall on me all consuming Fire watch me burn.

For me to truly love you, I must be with Him/Jesus. For only when I am lost in His love do I know who I am. For when I am lost in Jesus I am found in Him.

To love or not to love that is the question. To love is to be loved by the one who is love. God is love and God so loved me. John 3:16.

I will love because God so loved me.

God spells love JESUS and so do I.

(Big Boys Do Cry)

Big girls don't cry and real men don't cry? Well that's a lie!

Men, women, boys and girls can and should laugh and cry out loud! Why? Because we are all human with a heart. Tears show you have a heart and that you care. Tears of sorrow, tears of joy. Let it rain!

P.S. Tears clear your sinuses, so let it rain salty tears.
P.S.S. As a man I can express my feelings. My hearts cry in a tear or two million tears! Real men can cry a river and real women can be a tomboy princess with or without make up or hair pins!

Charles W. Warner

"*He gathers the lambs in his arms and carries them close to his heart*"

Isaiah 40:11

February 14, 2015 at 8:50am · Rockford, IL ·Happy Valentine's Day
Jesus
A love store/Psalm

(Feed My Sheep)

Do you love me? Feed my sheep.

Jesus I love you. I will feed your sheep, for I am your Bride. I am your dove and you are my love, I will love even as you are Love.

Lord may I love your sheep as you love your sheep of whom I am one.

Endow me with love and I will love.
Sing over me and I shall dance.
Infuse me with fire and authority and I will burn.

Empower me with passion and purpose and I will live.
Dear Lord Jesus you are my life, my world, my love song. My soul delights in you, my flesh cries out for my living God. For you alone hear my hearts cry.

Lord I hear you call me by name, I hear your heartbeat in the still of the night.

Abide here Lord God for I am yours and you are mine.

Charles W. Warner

(A Kitten's Prayer)

Dear Jesus,
When I am up all night, you are my light. My hearts delight. The one
I play with while burning the midnight oil.

When I sleep all day, in that cozy corner chair where I stay. I know
you watch over me, you are my dream giver.

Jesus, I pray, thank you for all your sweet love.
Jesus, you are my love. My Beloved one.

I also want to say thank you for my Family.

My dad, Felix.
My mom, Ginger.
My brother, Tony the tiger, lol, yeah right.
My sophisticated sister, Powder Puff.
And even bless Rover, (roll over Rover), my dog,
or I should say our brother.

Jesus we are a Family because you are our Big Brother. Jesus honestly you make life worth living.

P.S. Jesus you are this cat's meow!

Love from,

FurBall.

(Released)

There is something so amazing about the transformation process of a butterfly. They undergo the most remarkable cycle, a transformation that brings a beautiful freedom. But what's most amazing about the butterfly is that it never stays in the same stage forever. From a small egg a caterpillar is born, it eats and eats so it can grow quickly. Then it becomes a chrysalis, what we call the cocoon. This stage is so important to the caterpillar. It's where it will become great. Where it develops into the beautiful butterfly. If the caterpillar were to stay in its chrysalis stage forever it would never reach its full and beautiful destiny.

What would life be like without the beautiful butterfly? What would life be like if WE never emerge from our chrysalis stage?
Some of us have been staying in a place of safety, a place of comfort and a place of solitude. It's time to be released. It's time to be transformed. It's time to wear your colors. It's time to spread your wings. Jesus has more plans for you than staying within your cocoon. He's filled you with so much of Him it's time trust, to break out into your dreams. Your past does not define you, but it's brought you up to here. Jesus says you're lovely, he says he has great plans for you. Get ready to be released. Get ready to be transformed. Those dreams you've been dreaming, it's time to take ahold.

Rom 12:2 ...let God transform you into a new person by changing the way you think. Then you will learn to know Gods will for you, which is good and pleasing and perfect."

Angela Smith

(Butterfly Wings)

In my life I have learned there are many things I can live without,
love is not on that list.
Life without love is like a bird without feathers, a butterfly without
wings it's the saddest of things.

God is love. God is my Beloved One. He delights in me.

I will live
I will love
I will sing
I will dance
I will fly

Forever more because

"God so loves me"
"Jesus is my joy"
"I feed on the fire of Holy Ghost"

I am my Beloved and He is mine.

~Song of the Butterfly~

My words, my songs are as honey from God's heart sweet words,
sweet songs sung over people.

Charles W. Warner

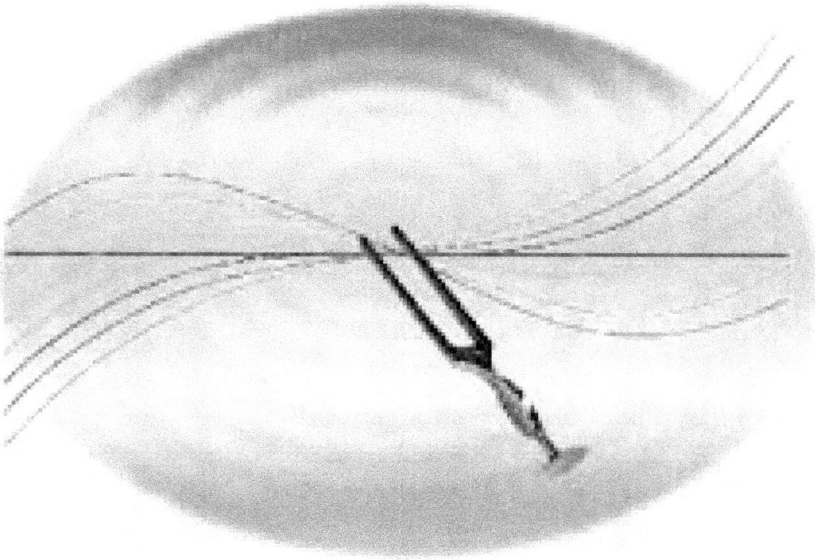

(Tuning Fork)

I am a tuning fork in the hand of God.

I will make a joyful noise resounding the songs of Heaven

My molecules are in motion to the glory of God.
My D.N.A. will say blessed be God forever.
My heart beat resonates as a tribal drum
I am a live wire Holy Ghost is the Fire.

Charles W. Warner

(Wicked Woman)

Based on Proverbs chapter 7

Young man do not walk by her home. She looks young and fair but she is the Devil's Daughter! She will entice you with the finest wines, she will wrap silk chains around your soul, and she will promise you Heaven and give you nothing but Hell. She will say~ I am bored and lonely, I am innocent, won't you come into my chamber? All the while weaving you into her wicked web to drag your sorry soul to the pits of hell! Warning do not go by her home or down her street for she has sisters, fellow Hell Spawns.

Charles W. Warner

Proverbs 7:6-27

New King James Version (NKJV)

The Crafty Harlot

6 For at the window of my house
I looked through my lattice,
7 And saw among the simple,
I perceived among the youths,
A young man devoid of understanding,
8 Passing along the street near her corner;
And he took the path to her house
9 In the twilight, in the evening,
In the black and dark night.

10 And there a woman met him,
With the attire of a harlot, and a crafty heart.
11 She was loud and rebellious,
Her feet would not stay at home.
12 At times she was outside, at times in the open square,
Lurking at every corner.
13 So she caught him and kissed him;
With an impudent face she said to him:
14 "I have peace offerings with me;
Today I have paid my vows.
15 So I came out to meet you,

Diligently to seek your face,
And I have found you.
16 I have spread my bed with tapestry,
Colored coverings of Egyptian linen.
17 I have perfumed my bed
with myrrh, aloes, and cinnamon.
18 Come, let us take our fill of love until morning;
Let us delight ourselves with love.
19 For my husband is not at home;
He has gone on a long journey;
20 He has taken a bag of money with him,
And will come home on the appointed day."
21 With her enticing speech she caused him to yield,
With her flattering lips she seduced him.
22 Immediately he went after her, as an ox goes to the
slaughter,
Or as a fool to the correction of the stocks,[a]
23 Till an arrow struck his liver. As a bird hastens to the
snare, He did not know it would cost his life.
24 Now therefore, listen to me, my children;
Pay attention to the words of my mouth:
25 Do not let your heart turn aside to her ways,
Do not stray into her paths;
26 For she has cast down many wounded,
And all who were slain by her were strong men.
27 Her house is the way to hell,
descending to the chambers of death.

1 Corinthians 6:13

Now the body is not for sexual immorality but for the Lord, and the Lord for the body.

1 Corinthians 6:15-17
15 Do you not know that your bodies are members of Christ? Shall I then take the members of Christ and make them members of a harlot? Certainly not! 16 Or do you not know that he who is joined to a harlot is one body with her? For "the two," He says, "shall become one flesh." 17 But he who is joined to the Lord is one spirit with Him.

(The Old Rugged Cross)

On a hill far away stood an old rugged cross,
the emblem of suffering and shame;
and I love that old cross where the dearest and best
for a world of lost sinners was slain.

So I'll cherish the old rugged cross,
till my trophies at last I lay down;
I will cling to the old rugged cross,

and exchange it some day for a crown.

O that old rugged cross, so despised by the world,
has a wondrous attraction for me;
for the dear Lamb of God left his glory above
to bear it to dark Calvary.

In that old rugged cross, stained with blood so divine, a wondrous
beauty I see,
for 'twas on that old cross Jesus suffered and died,
to pardon and sanctify me.

To that old rugged cross I will ever be true,
its shame and reproach gladly bear;
then he'll call me some day to my home far away,
where his glory forever I'll share.

George Bennard, 1873-1958
"It was not nails that kept Jesus on the cross
His love held Him there"

*I am but dust in the wind yet with God I am clay in the hands of The
Master Potter. All Consuming Fire, Refiners Fire mold me and make
me ever new for all I want to be is just like you!*

I will run all my days with my Daddy.
I will lean on His everlasting arm,
*I will forever run into The Fire into my Daddy's arms and be
consumed for this is why I live.*
*May we shine forth His glory and live out His love now and in that
great forever more...*

Charles W. Warner

(The Lighthouse)

There's a lighthouse on the hillside
That overlooks the sea
When I'm tossed it sends out a light
That I might see
And the light that shines in darkness now
Will safely lead me o'er
If it wasn't for the lighthouse
My ship would be no more

(Narrative)
It seems that everybody about us says
Tear that old lighthouse down
The big ships just don't pass this way anymore
So there's no use in standing around
Then my mind goes back to that one dark, stormy night
When just in time, I saw the light
Yes, it was the light form that old lighthouse
That stands up there on the hill

And I thank God for the lighthouse
I owe my life to Him
Jesus is the Lighthouse
And from the rocks of sin
He has shown a light around me
That I might clearly see
If it wasn't for the lighthouse
Tell me where would this ship be?

I thank God for the lighthouse
I owe my life to Him
Jesus is the Lighthouse
And from the rocks of sin
He has shown a light around me
That I might clearly see
If it wasn't for the lighthouse
Tell me where would this ship be?

Words and Music by Robbie Hinson
1971

(Blessed Assurance)

Blessed assurance, Jesus is mine!
O what a foretaste of glory divine!
Heir of salvation, purchase of God,
Born of His Spirit, washed in His blood.

This is my story, this is my song,
Praising my Savior, all the day long;
This is my story, this is my song,
Praising my Savior, all the day long.

Perfect submission, perfect delight,
Visions of rapture now burst on my sight;
Angels descending bring from above
Echoes of mercy, whispers of love.

Perfect submission, all is at rest
I in my Savior am happy and blest,
Watching and waiting, looking above,
Filled with His goodness, lost in His love.

Words: Fanny Crosby, 1873:

(My Beloved)

I am God's Princess, Jesus Bride. As I live, and move and have my being, Holy Spirit sets me to flame. Holy Fire, All-consuming Fire, Refiners Fire dances in me, on me, surrounds me, goes before me, camps about me. Setting the elements and hearts ablaze. Even as I sleep, this Raging Fire lives, moves and has its being taking territories for the glory of God. For the Kingdom of God. For I am a Daughter of God. "I am a live wire and Holy Ghost is The Fire."

God may we be set to flame, to fly high. To set this world a blaze with wild fire. For we are only here a few short days. "Speak truth, live, love."

Charles W. Warner

Artist~ Jennifer Treece

(The Wedding)

Not too long ago I had a dream. Charlie and I are getting married on December 27th, only a few weeks away from now. Our families are close and his sister Nancy is my best female friend. Charlie is my best friend too. Anyways in my dream I was wearing my wedding dress and Charlie and I were about to get married. It came time and I noticed that I had nobody to give me away. I remember saying that my Dad isn't here anymore and that there isn't anyone to do so .I could see Charlie and knew there were others there but I didn't actually see them. I knew that there were quite a few. I was feeling a bit sad and missing my father when God appeared. He told me that He was my Father and that He would give me away. I remember that He was very tall, so tall that I couldn't see his face. He wore glowing white clothes as a bright light I have never before seen. I looked up and there was a balcony and in it there were many people up in Heaven, but I could only see my dad. He was watching and I could feel his happiness. My heart felt so full and loved that God would do this for me and bring my dad and Charlie's mom, Kay to our wedding. For Charlie's mom was also in the balcony but on the other side of God above Charlie so I could not see her, but Charlie could and he was looking up at her as I looked at my dad. The balcony of Heaven. I was so happy as I took God's hand and he placed it in my new husband's own hand and we became one under and by God with our parents in attendance, not to mention they had the best seats. Warmth and peace radiated with love. I knew it was blessed by God His son Jesus and Holy Spirit to have experienced this and the blessings on our marriage are many. God is so great.

Connie Warner

(Glory Bus)

My Family and Friends were at a wonderful concert. Filled to overflowing with the glory, the sweet presence of God. The house was filled with my peeps, my singers Kari Jobe, Misty Edwards, Natalie Grant, 3rd Day, Keith Green, Steve Green, Carly Moore and many more. They were singing in the concert hall, the house of prayer. It was wonderful, resting and celebrating with my peeps, my Family, my God! This concert hall, house of prayer was a cave full of light and love.

The rocks themselves glistened and glowed. Resound, radiated and echoed the joy of Jesus. I know I touched the rock wall that flowed with Living water and it touched me. I felt power, joy love. It was older than time, ancient yet ever new. It brought me to my knees

while lifting my spirit high to Heaven, to the very heart of God. I tell
you the truth, this Rock is alive.

This Stone wall is the Rock of Ages, cleft for me, for you and the
water is Living Water! He touched me and smiled and said "I belong
here in His house here in His Heart."

I enjoyed the concert with my Family. After a while we split up to go
to lunch in Chicago. I got back and was so sad. The concert is over
and no one is there. I see a man that was dancing and singing on
stage. He was so alive in the joy of Jesus. He was working on the
sound board. I went up to him and I said "hello". He was like, "well
hello there." I said the concert is over (sad eyes). He said, with an
arm around my shoulder, "It's over just for now". I said" I'm sorry
but I'm lost and I can't find my Family." He says," you were lost, but
now you're found. You where blind, but now you see. You are holy,
on holy ground. Son of God. Your Family is in the dear care of God,
your Family is in the hand, the heart of God. We are about to leave
and are going your way. So, get on board. Soon I was in the front
seat talking. I asked him "how much do I owe?" and he roared in
laughter and said" paid in full". Looking in my eyes, he said, "Jesus
paid in your behalf. "I asked him" may I pray for you?" He says,
"Yes, please do so." I prayed this~
"What I have, I give to you. What you have, I receive.
To worship God,
to celebrate Jesus.
To love one another.
Led and fed by Holy Ghost."
He drinks in the prayer, saying he receives this. Saying yes, I am a
Heart Scribe. I hear God's Heartbeat. Writing it down, singing it out.
Now even at this same time I receive from him heavenly songs of
old to be sung anew for such a time as this. For this day and this
hour, songs just for me and songs for us all. For in this impartation it
is I and an angel!

The angel says~ now enjoy your friends, your peeps, your fellow singers. This is a glory bus! I look back and the bus is full of light. A glory cloud fills the air. There are songs, laughter and love all around. I run back there. I am drowned there. I start to introduce myself and I am drowned in "Welcome Charlie!!!" So I sing with Kari Jobe. (Swing Low Sweet Chariot coming forth to carry me home). Singing with all I am, home, home sweet home, in worship love and laughter. All too soon I am dropped off at my home in Rockford, Illinois. I am sad to leave," please don't leave me alone, please don't stop the music, the dance, the laughter, the love." I cry." How can I leave where my heart lives?"

God comes to me, I drop to my knees in a pool of tears of joy, shaking like a leaf. He surrounds me and says~ "I Am with you. I Am always with you, my sweet child. My son. Hear me, this concert shall never die. It shall forever increase! Charlie you have caught my eye and touched my heart with your great hunger to know me and to bless me. I am with you. Rest, celebrate and dance to the music. Today, this day, sing for you are in the band!!! Yes, you are in the concert of the ages. This life in time is but a blink. Soon and very soon, you will be home in Heaven singing and celebrating in the halls of Heaven. Skipping down streets that are golden with your Family, your peeps and with me. For we are one in the Son. In Jesus we are forever Family, Best peeps forever."

Charles W. Warner

(My Poet's Heart)

Tender and sweet, a heart full of love. Honest words and a directive from God, he pens the words, the verses straight from our Father's heart.

A tender soul hurt before, wanting to be loved and understood for who he is. Simple and pure desires are what he needs for life.

He is a man of many talents and a heart of gold. He doesn't need much to be happy. He isn't complicated. A man who walks with God and isn't ashamed to share God's love and what Jesus has done.

Proud to be a Christian and to proclaim it by his written words, his spoken words and his actions.

A man with a love for nature and the outdoors. God's landscape. A stick and a stone, a cup of tea and a full tummy and he is content.

Not one to complain though he can be stubborn at times but he holds onto truth and loves big.

His expression is in his words, written on a page or shown in an action.

He loves me I know. Not by words does he always show it. He shows it in the many ways that make him the wonderful man I love.

He is beautiful inside and out. With eyes like twin pools of amber fire lighting the window to his soul. A soul on fire, Holy Spirit fire and it shows.
A seer and one who gets directives from our awesome God. Mantles given, dreams and visions and an insight only from God. He loves Jesus and even our wedding rings are special in what they proclaim.

I may not always show it and I am learning as he is to be one and have a marriage designed by God. I am his helpmate and he is mine "The husband being the Godly leader of the home is to also be the servant of all in the home~ to be like Jesus the servant King".
Connie Warner

27/12/2014

(In the Garden with Jesus)

I was reading a book and putting the book down to go into the kitchen to get a bite to eat. I prayed- Jesus I want to pray with you, to intercede with you, to see what you see, to hear what you hear, to know what you know. To hear your heart beat and fall at your feet in prayer and worship- and next thing I know, I am with Jesus on the Mount of Olives in the Garden of Gethsemane the night before he died (The sights, the sounds, the smell of the cool of the night) and He said slowly, gently yet ever so powerfully (looking in my eyes, my heart, my very soul) Will you.... pray with me? .... with Holy Ghost chill bumps and huge tears in my eyes I said," if you will be with me in this in prayer I will"- Jesus said," yes I am with you always. You are my inheritance and I am your inheritance we are one." P.S. I can't tell you what I went into the kitchen to eat, yet I can tell you what/who I found- Bread of Life and Living Water So now I pray, I intercede, I travel in prayer with Jesus and in this I often gets dreams and visions, poetry, prophetic writings and trips to Heaven. God said to me today while sleeping," Charles don't ever think your poetry, your writing is common place. Charles I give you words, treasures from my heart to feed the hungry hearts." All hearts are hungry and only Jesus satisfies a hungry heart. It's good to be hungry to seek after the Lord, to share the passion of Jesus, to have a heart that loves that only He can give.

Charles W. Warner

(Redemption)

Am I strong? No I am weak, yet I am well enough to know I need Jesus in every area of life. Without Jesus I am lost, my life is worthless gain, I am building my own castle just to watch it fall. Oh how I need Jesus every hour of every day. Jesus is my joy my strength and my salvation.

I need to be loved
I need the truth
I need wisdom
I need understanding
I need grace
I need glory salvation story.

In all things I can say-
I need Jesus
Who do you need?

Charles W. Warner

(Prophetic Flame)

My Wife is a Butterfly, Prophetic is She.

Connie, you are a prophetic artist, a butterfly learning to fly. Not always what is taught, more like what is caught in the school of the Holy Ghost, you know? Well written, deep and prophetic and yet simple and to the point.
Love is give and take. Often give and give
and knowing, when you give, its God that gives back. In speaking to hearts, press down, over flowing, running over.

You are a forever Princess of God
a butterfly finely formed and fashioned by her Creator
the one who speaks to your heart, heart to heart.

To hear to know, to see to be, eyes to see, ears to hear a love story
written so well by the one who is love.
Love has captured me in a cell of silk held together by grace
Set me on fire, yes watch me burn, for Lord all I truly want is to be
more like you!

For Lord my God, what have I got apart from you but a cage of my
own making? A dark cage, colder than ice, sharper than steel and
yet oh Lord my God I am not alone for you love me with an
everlasting love, even sending your Son in my behalf to be my
Savior.

Oh Lord my Lord how majestic is your name in all thee earth.

My God I will sing the glory of your name forever more for you saved me from me and you call me your Beloved one and I call you my All in ALL Amen...

Connie Frances Greene I know you have been cheated on, lied to and mistreated.

When will you be loved? God loves you and so do I. Know this, you are most loved by your Bride Groom even this day and forever and ever more. You are His precious, adorable Bride .His Beloved one. He gives you the desire of your heart's cry.

Connie Greene we knew each other since high school. You moved to North Carolina and Miami for a time, two bad marriages, and miscarriage from husband abuse. A cheating husband and a divorce. So you moved back here and moved in with my Dad and I. You were going to pay high rent to a slum lord in a damp hole in the wall. My Dad and I talked and said you can move in here. It just all fell together or else I should say a divine design.

May you and yours be blessed and highly favored

A man or woman in themselves does not complete you, only when Jesus is your all in all are you completed in Him. Only when life is orchestrated by God is it a wonderful life.

Honesty a relationship is bondage, a real ball and chain without God. Without God being first in all things. When God is first and worshiped then it can and will be a beautiful story that only He can write.

Charles W. Warner

(Jesus with Me)

Jesus, my sweet Jesus, Oh how I love thee.
Dear Jesus you saved me from me.
Dear Jesus I will wash your feet with my tears. I will anoint your feet
with oil and incense.
I will dry your feet with my hair.

Jesus, just to gaze in your eyes and fall at your feet means
everything to me, for you are my All in All.
"My Adonai".

Pour out on me as an anointing oil your sweet presence with me.
Wash over this vessel from the inside out
Fill this cup to overflow.

Deeper & deeper
Higher & higher

Love without limits

Saturate
My heart
My hands
My feet
My hair

I am yours dear Lord. Lavish me with your love, never let me go for
we are one.
Where you go, I go. Where you stay, I stay.
I am my Beloved and He is mine.

We are each one drop, but oh how He loves us all.

One drop in the Master's Hand is much more than an endless ocean without Him.

He is the sea and to be lost in Him is to be truly found in His Heart of love.

If there is anything lovely about me, it's because Jesus is the Beautiful One. Blessed be God forever.

With every breath I take
with ever move I make
with every heartbeat
I live my life to worship at my God's feet.

Charles W. Warner

(Fishers of Men)

Matt 4:18-23

"Come and follow me and be ye Fishers of men"

Cast your bait onto the waters and be ye Fishers of men.

In Jesus and with Jesus I am a fisher of men.
I have my fishing poles.
I have my set lines and I have my great casting net.

The Gospel, The Good-News is the bait that I use, for we are all hungry and only Jesus satisfies a hungry heart. Only the Holy Spirit awakens a dead heart to know its greatest need is Jesus.

I use my God given talents to cast The Gospel near and far out into the sea of the world.
God gave me the talents, the heart, the love to set the nets with Truth, with Fruit of the Holy Ghost, with The Gospel, The Good-News of our Lord Jesus.

One example of a talent God blessed me with is;

My books are bait
Holy Spirit and I cast this bait near and far
To hook hearts
To draw hearts home to Jesus.

Cast your bait onto the waters and be ye Fishers of men.

So I ask you, what is your God given talent/s that you are casting into the sea of life? Don't hide your light, don't bury your talents.

Shine bright for Jesus is our light and our love forever more.

Warn the sinner that the bridge is out!!! Warn the sinner of their need of Jesus, we all need Jesus. The truth, the Gospel is not hate speech, to remain silent would be hateful.

Never water down the Gospel to appease people. The Good news is meant to bring conviction onto repentance. Lukewarm is pacified religion! Let's be all the more on fire with a living relationship with God!!!

Go tell it on the mountains, over the hills and everywhere.
Go tell it on the mountains that Jesus Christ is Lord.

Charles W. Warner

Follow Me
and I will make you fishers of men.
Matthew 4:19

(My Hero)

To the God who
loves his creation so much
that he sent his only son. To
live among us and to take
upon himself every sin
mankind has ever acted out-
to be punished,
tortured, beaten, mocked,
rejected, pierced, and nailed
to a cross. A horrific death.
To be given what should've
been mankind's
punishment. To die for even
those who still to this day,
deny his existence, deny his
love, and deny his
cry "Father, forgive them,
for they know not what
they do" THAT's the hero I
want to know:-) (J.E.S.U.S)

It was not nails that kept Jesus on the cross
His love held Him there.

(Jesus Take the Wheel of My Heart)

~In a dream~

I find myself riding a silverback hog, a Harley Davidson street hog. Lined with leather and chrome, streaked with flames and lighting with the roar of thunder! I ride up into Bible study/home group with a yell" wooooh whoooooo yaaaahh", doing a wheelie ripping up grass doing figure eights. I finally proceed to park but not before doing a few donuts. Peeps are going "nice ride, yahhh", and on and on. I smile and eat it up.

Walking around the backyard where I parked, I see a man with grass stained overalls and grease covered hands I think nothing of it. I go to Bible study. On my way out I see my bike is gone. I look around and this self-same man is at a blast furnace proceeding to burn my bike! I run up to him and say "hello, what are you doing? This is my bike!" He says with a calm, sweet yet powerful voice," Charlie I am burning this bike."

I say "What?! Well you are going to have to buy me a new one!You need to be a witness and represent me ok?" He says "Charles, I Am always your Representative and Witness" I was like "What??? Sooooo, I am getting a new bike then?" He said "Yes, a brand new one. Old and yet ancient, older than time but yet ever new." I shake my head as chills run down my spine. I can't keep a smile off my face, I laugh and when I open my eyes I see a bike, I see my bike. It is simple yet powerful. I said "thank you .Will we meet again?" He says with a belly laugh, "oh yes indeed we shall meet again."

I drive my bike. I see a thin, mysterious man dressed in black with a cigar leaning on his polished 1970's Cadillac. He sees me and says "please dear sir, park here, Mr. VIP! You go right ahead Sir and take this most honored, prestige's parking space. You go ahead take what you want, take what is rightfully yours, be your own man take your life, take your girl. I am not here to take from you. I have my life. I have what I want, now go take what you want, do it your way." He says," nice bike now you need a mask, a helmet to go with your bike." He opens his truck and there it is, a million masks/helmets. He says pick a helmet to match your charm. lol .I look around thinking who am I?The ant eater, the chicken, the pig, the snake? He says "pick who you are. But I tell you you're no ant eater, your well above that. Come up higher my friend stand with me. Be a hell raiser! No the best is the hell spawn! This is who you can be, feed on my fire!!! hahaha !"

Then a thought came to my head my heart. Remember the tree of the knowledge of good and evil. Remember the story of Adam and Eve. So I stop and I ask, God Father God, Daddy who am I?

God thee Ancient of days, the Great I Am comes to me as a man with grass stained overalls and grease covered hands! He says" I Am the God of Abraham, Isaac, Jacob and Charlie."

He says" Son, My Beloved Son you are not one of those characters, you are not a want to be, you do not have to wear a mask for you have your Fathers eyes and your Daddy's heart .Who are you? You are mine and I am yours. Charles you have many mantles, gifts and talents. Remember this, you're first and foremost title will forever be Son for we are one."

Charles W. Warner

(Walking as Children Of Light)

By John Paul Jackson

I/We love and miss you Dear Brother John Paul Jackson we will meet you in Heaven in that great forever more till then we celebrate Jesus together always Amen.

As followers of Jesus, we need to develop a heightened sensitivity to the Lord and abide in His Word. When we do, we will hear God's voice just by walking with Him. We will see, hear, know, and understand God's ways and His heart.

Scripture tells us that as we abide in Him, we are transformed into His glorious image little by little (2 Corinthians 3:18). In fact, we become agents of transformation that advance the Kingdom of Light in the earth.

Although we carry the light of Christ within us, many of us fail to recognize the exciting spiritual impact we have on others. We become distracted by the little things in life, unaware of how God's light within us challenges the darkness around us.

Much of the time, we are focused only on those things which are seen (2Corinthians 4:18) and limit our thinking to what is logical, rational, or tangible. This is a two-dimensional mind-set that originated with Aristotle and that ignores the reality of the spiritual universe. In life, there are actually seven dimensions of reality: height, depth, width, soul, spirit, time, and light. To have a seven-dimensional mind-set is to embrace the reality of the supernatural.

As children of the light, the Lord allows us glimpses into the supernatural arena. Such revelations often motivate us to live holy

lives and restore our understanding of how awesome God is.

A few years ago, the Lord allowed me to "see" into the life of a young lady as she was moving from one apartment to another. I not only saw what was going on in the natural realm, but I was able to "see" what was going on in the spiritual realm where I saw both the hordes of hell and the heavenly hosts. For several hours one day, I watched God's angels and Satan's demons interacting in this woman's life. The Lord opened my eyes to "see" the Holy Spirit leading and guiding this young woman, placing thoughts and feelings into her heart and in her mind, although she was totally unaware of His presence.

In this vision, the young woman made a decision to sign an apartment contract and began moving into a new apartment. As she turned the doorknob and walked inside, I heard screams of fear from demons because light was entering the darkness.

Then, the young woman walked next door to use her neighbor's telephone. When the neighbor opened the door and saw the young woman, light entered into the neighbor. The Spirit of God within this young woman was impacting the neighbor.

The young woman wasn't thinking, "I feel the Holy Spirit's anointing on me." She wasn't even considering thoughts of evangelism or wondering if her neighbor was a Christian. Instead, she was embarrassed about knocking on her neighbor's door and she was grumbling under her breath about how much she hated moving. She was totally unaware of the spiritual impact she was having on her neighbor. She was simply going through the chores of everyday life, feeling more of its drudgery.

Later, I watched as the young woman drove to a grocery store. Passing by one store, she became frustrated with herself and wondered why she didn't see it in time. She began to look for a place to make a U-turn, but she saw a sign that prohibited U-turns. So she continued driving until she found another grocery store.

Entering the store, the young woman grabbed a shopping cart and began walking down the aisles, oblivious to the angels who were walking beside her. They were directing her shopping cart down the aisles in a haphazard pattern. However, the young woman felt "lost" in the store. She couldn't seem to find the things she needed and began to feel disoriented. Suddenly, an angel whispered to her, "Here we go. Keep on walking."

Blinded to the reality of an alternative spiritual universe, the young woman had just walked past demons who were sitting on shelves screaming out in fear and panic because they were overcome by the light. Once she had filled her shopping cart with food and cleaning supplies, the young woman steered the cart toward a checkout lane. Suddenly, another shopper edged in front of her. Frustrated, the young woman became irritated, unaware that several angels had actually shoved the shopper ahead of her.

The angels were eager to steer the young woman over to a different cashier whom they had been preparing for a "God encounter." On that day, the young woman was the fourth Christian who came through this cashier's line -- the fourth time God's light had hit her that day. What the young woman didn't realize was that five more times, and the cashier would become a Christian. By then, the cashier would have encountered the light of God so that she would be able to realize her need to change.

The young woman, however, was unaware of heaven's strategy. In fact, she was still irritated about the rude shopper who cut in front of her. Tired and frustrated, the young woman looked at her watch. She was behind schedule and felt an urgency to get home. "I would have been home a lot quicker," she thought, "if that person hadn't pulled in front of me. I can't believe that I missed that first grocery store."

Sadly, the young woman was ignorant to how God was using her to advance His Kingdom. Nor did she realize that one day she would receive a heavenly reward for what happened in the cashier's life, simply because she carried God's presence and walked with Him.

As children of the light, these sorts of things happen to us every single day, but often we are unaware of them. Our spiritual sensitivity is dull. Focused on the natural realm, we concentrate on simply existing and surviving. Sadly, we miss savoring the exciting adventures God has prepared for us.

Scripture says that God is light (John 1:89; 8:12; 1 John 1:5) and we are children of light (Ephesians 5:8). Light always exposes and expels the things of darkness (Ephesians 5:13).

Many of us think we have to "feel" spiritual to "be" spiritual, and thus to have a spiritual impact on others. But in reality, it has nothing to do with how we "feel." It has everything to do with our relationship to Jesus Christ and that He comes to live in us. We are simply earthen vessel that carry the presence of God. As the spirit of the living God flows through us, we have a spiritual impact on everyone and everything around us.

God called us into His marvelous light in order to proclaim His praises (1 Peter 2:9). Everywhere we go, He will go with us

(Matthew 28:20; John 14:20-21). He will live in us. His light will emanate through us. His power and anointing will flow out from us, touching and changing everyone we come in contact with.

Remember, "It is God who commanded light to shine out of darkness, who has shone in our hearts to give the light of the knowledge of the glory of God in the face of Jesus Christ" (2 Corinthians 4:6).

(Love Letter)

"Do you know how loved you are My Bride? My every thought is of you, if you could count the thoughts I think toward you in one moment of time, they would be more than the grains of sand of all the oceans in the world. You are my delight. You are my desire. Come into My chambers, I long to shower you with my love. I long for our time alone. My heart beats with anticipation for the day I come to bring you to my Father's house. Soon my Bride, and you will see, all of heaven waits for that day.

I am coming for you My Bride, in a twinkling of an eye, you will be by my side."
~Jesus, your Bridegroom.

John 14: 1-3 KJV

(Sunset and Seasons of the Soul)

Yes I am in love with God.
I see and sense God.
In the sunset.
In the sunrise.
In a warm summer rain.
In a cold snowy night.
In the light of a hot day.
In the cool of a bright starry night.
In a spring flower, God I love you every hour.
In the brisk breeze.
In the autumn leaves.
God is in the sweet tea that you share with me.
God is in the seasons of the soul.

"God so loves"

Charles W. Warner

(I Am A Dancer)

Lord God set me on fire, your heart's desire burn in me.
All the colors of the rainbow, all the colors of your heart.
Set my feet to dance with the Lord of the Dance.
Sing over me a new song.
Anoint me with sweet incense.

Anoint me to dance in the desert and watch the desert grow. Flow Holy Spirit flow. Anoint me to see the dance floor glow. Lord may I glow, may I show forth your glory and live out your love.

Holy Ghost inhabit my heart/ our hearts.
Let the glory fall down.
Let embers of fire fall from us your dancers.
God blow that these embers will grow into a wild fire.

Living light. Wild fire live in me. Fall on me, fall on the dance floor, and fall on hearts. Inhabit our hearts and inhabit our feet to dance. To uplift Jesus the Lord of the dance.

Jesus is my joy.
So shall I live.
So shall I love.
So shall I sing
So shall I dance forever more.

Charles W. Warner

(Walking in God's Favor)

Calling forth giants in the natural and supernatural... Calling forth
giants from this fallen world...
Eyes to see and ears to hear...
Giants in Jesus!

Jesus is our joy...
Our dance in the day...
Our song in the night.
It is well, Emmanuel is with us.

I live, move and have my being in Christ Jesus.
I can do all things though Christ Jesus.

We are in the Army of the Lord most high...
Called to conquer, Called to take the land...
Taking the Kingdom by force.

Clam what is yours... Walk it out...Live it out!

Calling forth the wealth of the wicked into the Kingdom!

Calling the wicked into the Kingdom. Where they were among the most wicked in the enemy's camp. I call them forth they are righteous leaders in Jesus, walking in God's favor.

10X ,100X limitless in Gods Family. Isaiah 60: 1-2.

Hear the clarion call, one and all! Calling forth all saints, calling forth all angels! Hark the Herold angels sing all glory to the King of kings. The King of glory... Salvation's Story.

Calling forth the Kingdoms of this world...Calling forth the Nations of this world to become the Kingdom and Nations of our God and King.

Matthew 11:12 New King James Version (NKJV)

12 And from the days of John the Baptist until now the kingdom of heaven suffers violence, and the violent take it by force.

Romans 8:37-39 New King James Version

37 Yet in all these things we are more than conquerors through Him who loved us. 38 For I am persuaded that neither death nor life, nor angels nor principalities nor powers, nor things present nor things to come, 39 nor height nor depth, nor any other created thing, shall be able to separate us from the love of God which is in Christ Jesus our Lord.

Revelation 11:15 And the seventh angel sounded; and there were great voices in heaven, saying, The kingdoms of this world are become the kingdoms of our Lord, and of his Christ; and he shall reign for ever and ever.

King James Bible Habakkuk 2:14

For the earth shall be filled with the knowledge of the glory of the LORD, as the waters cover the sea.

Charles W. Warner

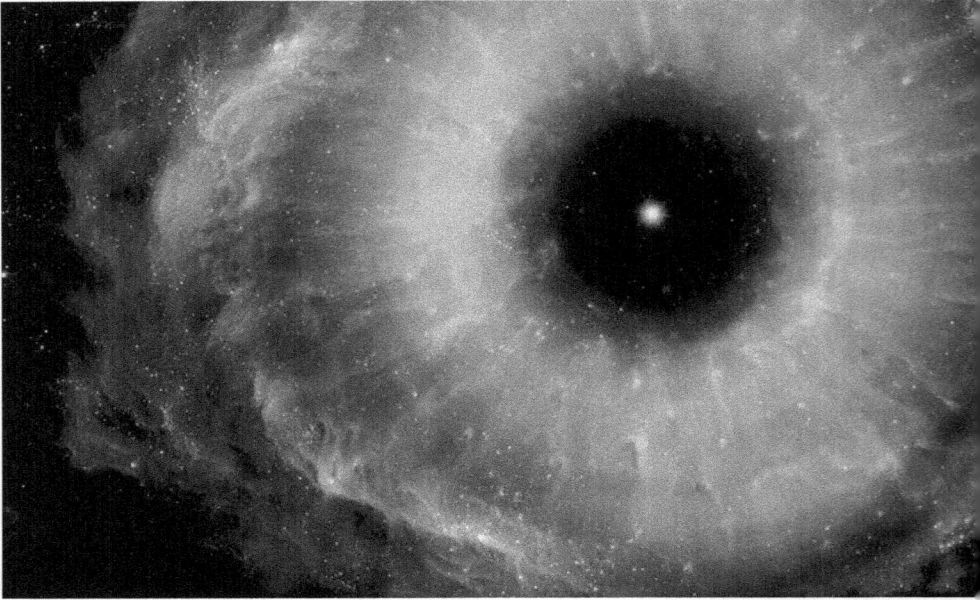

(Fear Not)

Fear not the ramblings of fools in their folly.

Evolution is a lie to be fed to fools
for the wise will not partake thereof
for the wise feed on the favor and friendship with God
not the accolades and camaraderie of mere mortal man.

Charles W. Warner

*Is 51:12 I, even I, am he that comforteth you: who art
thou, that thou shouldest be afraid of a man that shall die,
and of the son of man which shall be made as grass;*

Ps 14:1 The fool hath said in his heart, There is no God.

(Matthew Henry's Concise Commentary)

14:1-7 A description of the depravity of human nature, and the deplorable corruption of a great part of mankind. - The fool hath said in his heart, there is no God. The sinner here described is an atheist, one that saith there is no Judge or Governor of the world, no Providence ruling over the affairs of men. He says this in his heart. He cannot satisfy himself that there is none, but wishes there were none, and pleases himself that it is possible there may be none; he is willing to think there is none. This sinner is a fool; he is simple and unwise, and this is evidence of it: he is wicked and profane, and this is the cause. The word of God is a discerner of these thoughts. No man will say, There is no God, till he is so hardened in sin, that it is become his interest that there should be none to call him to an account. The disease of sin has infected the whole race of mankind. They are all gone aside, there is none that doeth good, no, not one. Whatever good is in any of the children of men, or is done by them, it is not of themselves, it is God's work in them. They are gone aside from the right way of their duty, the way that leads to happiness, and are turned into the paths of the destroyer. Let us lament the corruption of our nature, and see what needs we have of the grace of God: let us not marvel that we are told we must be born again. And we must not rest in anything short of union with Christ, and a new creation to holiness by his Spirit. The psalmist endeavors to convince sinners of the evil and danger of their way, while they think themselves very wise, and good, and safe. Their wickedness is described. Those that care not for God's people, for God's poor, care not for God himself. People run into all manner of wickedness, because they do not call upon God for his grace. What good can be expected from those that live without prayer? But those that will not fear God, may be made to fear at the shaking of a leaf. All our knowledge of the depravity of human nature should endear to us salvation out of Zion. But in heaven alone shall the whole company of the redeemed rejoice fully, and for evermore. The world is bad; oh that the Messiah would come and change its character! There is universal corruption; oh for the times of reformation! The triumphs of Zion's King will be the joys of Zion's children. The second coming of Christ, finally to do away the dominion of sin and Satan, will be the completing of this salvation, which is the hope, and will be the joy of every Israelite indeed. With this assurance we should comfort ourselves and one another, under the sins of sinners and sufferings of saints.

(My Living God)

Isaiah 44:9-11. All who make idols are nothing, and the things they treasure are worthless. Those who would speak up for them are blind; they are ignorant, to their own shame. 10 Who shapes a god and casts an idol, which can profit him nothing? 11 He and his kind will be put to shame; craftsmen are nothing but men. Let them all come together and take their stand; they will be brought down to terror and infamy.

Compared to eternity we were born yesterday, here today and gone tomorrow. What we do with the time we been given counts for eternity.

Time is a bubble and when eternity over takes time, what side of the cross will you be on? What you do with Jesus today will have everything to do with your future tomorrow, your eternal future.

(The Choice) Jesus is your Savior, Lord and Master by choice or else the devil is your Master by default!

Golden Idols and Sand Castles

In a world of shifting sinking sand Jesus and only Jesus is the Rock Of Ages.

Except the LORD build the house, they labour in vain that build it: except the LORD keep the city, the watchman waketh but in vain. Ps

Men worship money & women worship men with money.
Do not worship idols of silver and gold. Do not worship idols of flesh and blood.
Do not worship lust and lies, do not worship men for money or women for their long legs.
Do not worship movie stars, sport starts, rock stars or fast cars.
Do not worship the planets or the stars.
Only worship the Morning Star the Day Star, The Rock of Ages who is worthy of all praises.

The world wise the earthly rich try to own the world on the backs and bones of the saints, but they shall be cut down by the hand of God. They shall inherit the sands of the sea and the fires of hell! But not so with men whose trust is in the Lord. They shall inherit the earth and walk with God in the cool of the day.

Don't worship a carved stone, worship The Rock of Ages = (Jesus)
Charles W. Warner

(A Gardener's Hands)

Hands turned brown from the summer's sun. A little calloused and worn.

There's some dirt beneath the nails and they may not be all that pretty and neat. That is alright, for the gardener's passion is his love for his garden. For dirt and rock and rain, for every flower and plant. There is none too small or unimportant and all deserve and get his love and time. From the tiny weakly seedling that doesn't seem to grow, he tends day and night. Doing all he knows to do just to somehow help it survive. He chooses each plant carefully and decides exactly where it will go and when to plant it. Each spot is planned and prepared to cater to the life chosen to grow there. A life that will be coaxed and nurtured with love by the gardener's hands. Along with the sunshine, water and earth, it will grow into the beauty and bounty that God Himself planned out for it. From His own special gardens and the wisdom he implants on the hearts and minds of the gardener, the little garden will continue to grow and reach towards the sky and climb up to the heavens towards the Creator of us all. For both man and God enjoy the harvest and the joy it brings to the gardener and to all who behold its beauty. For God has blessed the gardener and we are all of His garden.

Connie Warner

(Balloons)

When I was 11 years old in 5th grade we had a balloon launch. We had little notes tied to the balloon strings saying" hello I live in Rockford, Illinois may I ask where you live?" To see how far this balloon traveled.

Now a days I send a massage high into the sky by prayers, the written Word, the spoken Word and in silent prayer that speaks oh so loud.

Holy Ghost is my Balloon that shall never ever lose His power. Holy Ghost is my Balloon and He is a mighty wind carrying the Good News around the world blessing the land and saving hearts. Fly, Holy Ghost, fly with fire in your wings and a song in your heart and I will fly with you for you are the wind beneath my wings and you will always be the song in my heart.

Charles W. Warner

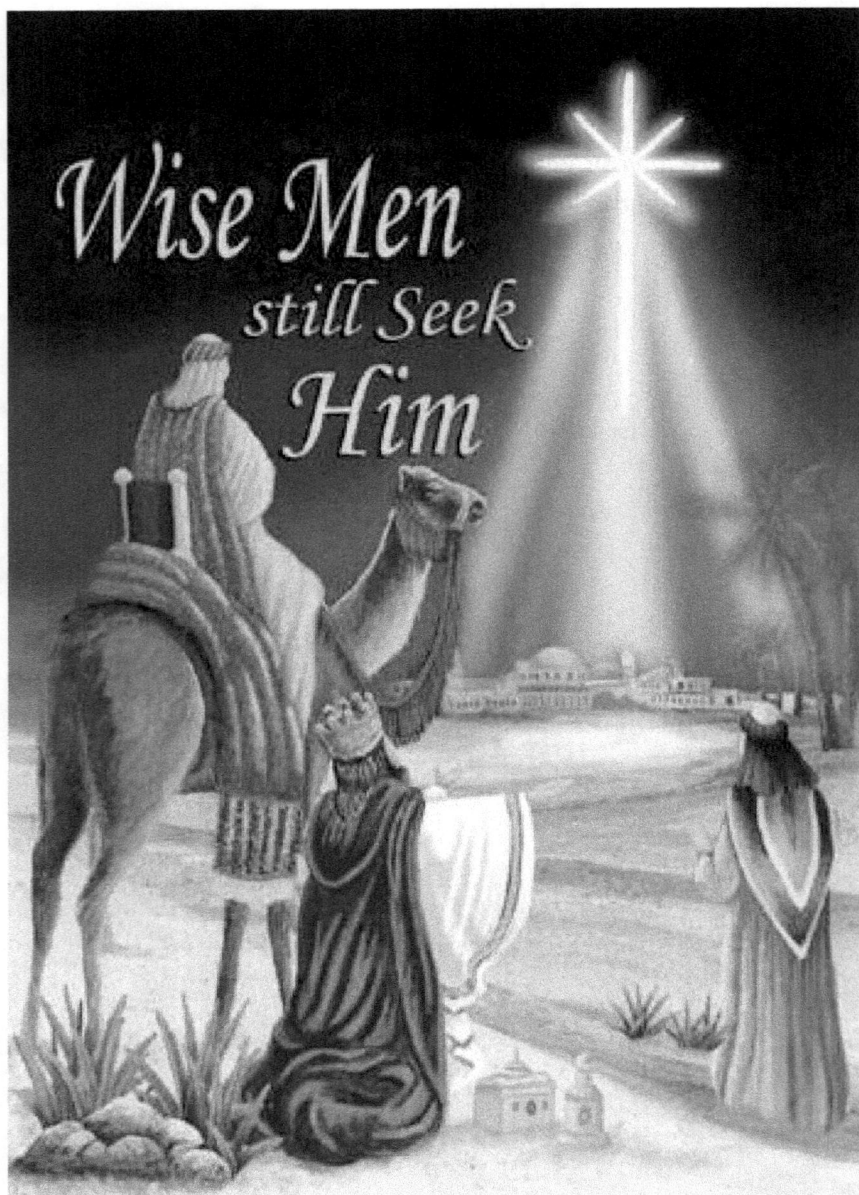

(Ruler of the Star's)

Ruler of all hear me as I call
Ruler of the day I know you hear me when I pray.
Lord help me in all I do and say.

Ruler of the night, by your might, help me be what is right in your sight.

Ruler of the stars,
Ruler of the sea,
Be Ruler of me.

Charles W. Warner

He became flesh and dwelt among us~ Immanuel God is with us.

"The presence of God is the greatest present of all"

Thank God for his Son- a gift too wonderful for words!
2 Cor 9:15

JESUS, The Greatest Gift of All Time

About The Author

Charles W. Warner lives with his wife, Connie and family in Rockford, Illinois. A family man, Charles always puts his family first after God as He has intended for us. He is a poet after God's own heart and it is his love for Jesus that gives him his inspiration and motivation. Charles is an active member of Faith Center Church in Rockford and serves the Lord through the church, his writings and several other projects. He is actively involved in the Beautification of Rockford group through the park district. He has planted several beautiful trees throughout the parks in Rockford and is an avid gardener. He also works with wood and has created many wooden walking sticks and canes as a part of his Forest City Walking Sticks. God first for him. He is currently working on a few new ideas for his

next books.